IS CALVINISM BIBLICAL?

A BIBLICAL EXAMINATION OF CALVINISM CONCERNING:

- SALVATION
- ELECTION
- PREDESTINATION

By Cooper P. Abrams, III
January, 2014

Disclaimer

The author of this work has quoted the writers of many articles and books. This does not mean that the author endorses or recommends the works of others. If the author quotes someone, it does not mean that he agrees with all of the author's tenets, statements, concepts, or words, whether in the work quoted or any other work of the author. There has been no attempt to alter the meaning of the quotes; and therefore, some of the quotes are long in order to give the entire sense of the passage.

Address All Inquiries To:
THE OLD PATHS PUBLICATIONS, Inc.
142 Gold Flume Way
Cleveland, Georgia, U.S.A. 30528

Web: www.theoldpathspublications.com
E-mail: TOP@theoldpathspublications.com

1.0

DEDICATION

- To my wife Carolyn who has been my faithful companion for over fifty years. She has kept me on track and encouraged me constantly. It meant so much to me when she would tell me how proud she was of me. Being a pastor's wife can be a difficult life to live, but she has remained faithful to the Lord and without her help and support none of the churches that God has used us to establish would exist. Carolyn, your reward will be seen at the BEMA in gold, silver, and precious stones, which will honor your Savior and Lord.

- To those who will read this book and be directed to God's Word and His Truth.

- To each of the five congregations I pastored and those who stood with me on God's Word and who overlooked my disabilities.

Cooper P. Abrams, III
January, 2014

FOREWORD

The false doctrines of Calvinism are making a resurgence in America and in many parts of the world. Anyone who has studied the subject knows how confusing it can sometimes be. Having known Dr. Cooper Abrams III for more than 35 years, I know him to be a godly man with a passion for the truth of God's Word. He has always been a proponent of proper biblical interpretation, not imposing his beliefs on the Bible but studying and drawing out of the Bible what is there to form the foundation of what every Christian should believe. This book is another example of Dr. Abram's candid, careful and correct examination of a false system of theology in light of Bible truth. He has made what is sometimes confusing very understandable for the ordinary Christian who longs for Bible truth.

Dr. Abrams includes key historical information about John Calvin himself which is both accurate and enlightening. He breaks down the teaching and claims of the Calvinistic system of theology and then examines key Bible passages that are often used to support Calvinism. You will read this book with great profit if you are searching for the plain Biblical truth concerning this subject. When I first read the original manuscript for this book I knew this needed to be in print. May our Lord give wide circulation to this excellent book.

Dr. Roger Baker
Calvary Baptist Bible College & Seminary
King, North Carolina
January, 2014

TABLE OF CONTENTS

TABLE OF CONTENTS

INTRODUCTION

IS CALVINISM BIBLICAL?

One of the Most Debated Subjects

For centuries, Calvinism has been one of the most debated subjects along with the doctrines of election and predestination as taught by the modern Reformed movement. The importance of the subject is manifest in that it deals directly with the doctrine of salvation by grace. These two doctrines are widely debated by professing Christians who have divided themselves into opposing camps of "Calvinists" and "Arminians." However, there is a third group that is often overlooked. This group is made up of those who accept neither of these extreme views and reject the tenets of both positions. It is the view of this group that will be explained and shown to be the biblical view. The scope of this work will only address the teachings of Calvinism which are the most radical and unbiblical view.

The True Biblist

Those who believe the Bible to be the inerrant and infallible Word of God will take its doctrines seriously. The true biblist[1] appeals to God's word to find His truth in the doctrines of predestation and election, freewill and human responsibility. He will insist, that based on God's word the truth of the matter can be absolutely discerned.

Understanding the Problem

To understand the problem, let us look at the various positions held, the terms used, and a brief history of the topic. This will present a biblical solution that correctly addresses the issue and avoids the unbiblical extremes of both the Calvinists and the Arminians. The purpose of this paper is not to present an exhaustive study of the subject, but rather to address the practical side of this theological system, pointing out its unbiblical flaws for the average believer in Jesus Christ.

CHAPTER ONE
INTRODUCTION TO CALVINISM

Calvinism is a System of Theology

Calvinism is a system of theology that is associated with the Protestant theologian John Calvin, a Frenchman, who later became a Swiss reformer (1509-1564). The term "Calvinism" refers to doctrines and practices that stemmed from his works. The tenets of modern Calvinism are based mainly on his classic work *Institutes of the Christian Religion* which was published in its final edition in 1559.[2] It would not be correct to state that John Calvin developed modern Calvinism; rather Calvinism is based on his work and has been expanded by his followers.

John Calvin

John Calvin was born in Noyon, a small town in Picardy, France in 1509. He was the youngest of four children, all boys. When Calvin was twelve years old his father, Gérard Cauvin (Calvin) sent him to the University of Paris to study theology. It was his father's desire since Calvin's childhood that he would study theology and become a priest in the Roman Catholic Church.[3]

His Education

At age twelve, around 1520 or 1521, Calvin began his education by attending the University of Paris. He received his licentiate[4] in arts and his master's degree. However, between 1528 and 1533, his father directed him to abandon his theological studies, and young Calvin worked on a more profitable law degree in the schools of Bourges and Orleans. Subsequently, Calvin completed his studies and was licensed to practice law.

Calvin's Transition

Calvin was raised as a devout Catholic, but it appears that he began to move toward Protestantism after reading Martin Luther's writings. There is no record of Calvin's actual conversion or his salvation, but he changed the direction of his studies from law back to theology in 1557.[5] His conversion seems to have consisted of a slow transition to becoming a Protestant sometime between 1529 or early 1530.[6] In Calvin writings, he emphasizes his gradual transition over time from Catholicism toward Protestant Christianity rather than a single event of conversion. He stated, "We are converted little by little to God, and by stages."[7] Clearly, Calvin did not accept conversion as an event in one's life in which one becomes a believer and is at that moment born again. Rather he described his conversion as a gradual evolution towards God. This element in his life casts a shadow over Calvin's actual salvation. The true state of his heart cannot be known, but insight can be gleaned from his writings, and most importantly, from his actions in Geneva. However, it should be noted, that there is no example in the New Testament that would support his idea of a gradual process of salvation.

Calvin, The Reformed Protestant

What is clear is that Calvin gradually moved from being a devout Roman Catholic to becoming a devoted Reformed Protestant. However, being converted to Protestantism is not the same thing as being truly converted and spiritually "born again." The Protestant Reformation was a reforming of Roman Catholicism, but it did not cleanse it from all its errors.

Problems With Protestantism

In reality, Protestantism retained much of the errors of Roman Catholicism such as a universal church, pedo-baptism, sacraments, sprinkling as a mode of baptism, and the church as a means of salvation as seen in the practice of ex-communication. It also continued the idea of the state being under the control (in varying degrees) of the church, along with a state paid clergy. There was never in the Protestant Reformation a clear break from Catholicism. Like all cults and false religions, Protestantism was founded not solely on the Bible (Sola Scriptura), but on the writings, opinions, ideas, and councils of churchmen as to what the Bible teaches or what they thought would be proper religion.

Swiss Protestantism and Anglicanism

Swiss Protestantism was founded by John Calvin and is the foundation of Presbyterianism; Martin Luther, founded Lutheranism; and Henry VII founded Anglicanism when he broke England away from the Roman Catholic Church. This was the same error that Jesus condemned the religious leaders of Israel for committing. Israel too followed the writings of the rabbis in the Talmud,[8] instead of the Torah (the Old Testament).

Calvin's "Institutes of the Christian Religion"

The modern Reformed movement is based on Calvin's *"Institutes of the Christian Religion"* and many of the teachings of the Institutes are not biblical.

CHAPTER TWO

WHAT DOES HISTORY RECORD OF JOHN CALVIN'S CHARACTER?

Calvin's View of His Role

It is easily seen in the writings of John Calvin that he considered himself as having a special calling from God. He believed that throughout his life he was following, with great dedication, God's will and was the faithful defender of truth. As the pastor of Geneva he saw his role as purging the city of immorality of all kinds. His method was to use the civil government as an arm of the church to establish correct and strict laws of behavior, but also as executing judgment and punishments of offenders.

A man's true character can be seen in what he does, and not necessarily by what he says. Calvin is lauded as the greatest of Protestant theologian, and his *"Institutes of the Christian Religion"* is praised as a great work and a foundation of Reformed Protestant theology. There can be no misunderstanding that Calvin had a great respect and biblical fear of God. However, the extremes and false conclusions of this theology can certainly be questioned and shown to be unbiblical.

Calvin Based His Theology on the OT Law

Calvin based his theology almost solely on applying the Old Testament law, given to the Nation of Israel, to Christianity. He ignored the many passages in the New Testament and that plainly state that Christians, in this dispensation, are not under the law. Paul stated,

> *"For sin shall not have dominion over you: for ye are not under the law, but under grace." (Romans 6:)*[9]

He further explained,

> *"But now we are delivered from the law, that being dead wherein we were held; that we should serve in newness of spirit, and not in the oldness of the letter." (Romans 7:6)*

There can be no question that Calvin misunderstood that the law was given as their constitution and represented both spiritual and civil law to the nation of Israel. God never intended the law to apply literally to Christians. The principles behind the laws apply to all ages, and in our age, the principles are kept willingly by born again believers, not out of compulsion, but out of a love of God, His word, and righteousness.

Calvin Burned Witches at the Stake

John Calvin had those whom he thought were witches burned at the stake. However, Christians apply the principle behind God telling Israel not to allow a witch to live, by having nothing to do with witchcraft or anything associated with the occult.(See Exod. 22:18) The law in Exodus 22:18 was a civil law given to the Nation of Israel to protect its people from the occult. Paul made it clear that Christians are not to follow the letter of the law saying,

> *"But now we are delivered from the law,*

22

> *that being dead wherein we were held;*
> *that we should serve in newness of spirit,*
> *and not in the oldness of the letter."*
> *(Romans 7:6)*

The Apostle further explained,

> *"But now being made free from sin, and*
> *become servants to God, ye have your*
> *fruit unto holiness, and the end*
> *everlasting life." (Romans 6:22)*

Speaking of the freedom from the yoke of bondage of the law that the believer has in Christ Paul wrote,

> *"Stand fast therefore in the liberty*
> *wherewith Christ hath made us free, and*
> *be not entangled again with the yoke of*
> *bondage." (Galatians 5:1)*

This doctrinal truth escaped Calvin's reasoning and he incorrectly and relentlessly applied the civil law of Israel to the citizens of Geneva.

Calvin's Obsession

It is helpful in understanding Calvin's actions, that as the senior minister of Geneva, it was his obsession to purify the citizens of city from all immoral behavior. He thought that applying the law of Moses was the solution to the problem of sinful behavior. However, in looking at the actions of John Calvin, it can be plainly seen that his theology, was based on Augustinian thought, and was administered in a tyrannical, vindictive, cruel, and unloving way. It is difficult to find in the many hundreds of books written about John Calvin many instances of him being a loving, kind, merciful, or caring man, or pastor. He ruled and lorded over his congregation and using the civil authorities brought swift judgment on dissenters, even unto death.

In 1538, Calvin was forced to leave Geneva because of his unpopular views. Later in 1541, he was invited back. He was at first reluctant to return because of the opposition he had faced. What changed his mind was that those governing the city offered him lucrative benefits and position if he would return. The city was in turmoil, and they offered Calvin great power that he could exercise in his new office as the minister to Geneva. Their aim was to restore order to the troubled city. This power would allow him to,

> ". . . establish discipline and control behavior throughout the city."[10]

Calvin the Dictator

Calvin drafted ecclesiastical ordinances that created the constitution for the Reformed Church of the city-state of Geneva.[11] The Consistory, one of the three governing bodies of the city, had the jurisdiction over the enforcement of Calvin's laws. Calvin set about in earnest to remolding Geneva into a "City of God."[12] Harkness states,

> "It was the duty of the State, Calvin thought, to use its powers-if need be, its sword-bearing arm- to enforce moral living and sound doctrine."[13]

According to Harkness, "Before his death Calvin became virtually the civil as well as the ecclesiastical dictator of Geneva."[14] Calvin's grave error was in thinking that applying civil law, he could change the moral condition of the citizens of Geneva. Like every attempt to legislate morally, it miserably failed. If he had truly been a man of God he would have sought to bring spiritual revival to the city by preaching the saving Gospel of Jesus Christ as the only way to change the sinner's nature and life. When the sinner repents of his sins, God changes his nature and he becomes a moral and spiritual person. Calvin could not have understood 2 Corinthians 5:17, which says,

> *"Therefore if any man be in Christ, he is a new creature: old things are passed away; behold, all things are become new,"*

and taken the misguided course he pursued.

CHAPTER THREE

ATROCITIES FOR WHICH JOHN CALVIN WAS RESPONSIBLE

The Michael Servetus Case

The truth of the character of Calvin can be seen in the heretic Michael Servetus and others who were accused of violating his laws. Servetus was a scholarly theologian, and a renowned physician. He was condemned as a heretic by both the Roman Church as well as the Protestants for his rejection of the Trinity and infant baptism. In 1531, Servetus published a book titled "Errors of the Trinity" in which he referred to those who believed in the Trinity as believing in three Gods. He and Calvin corresponded for some time, but Servetus would not accept Calvin's teachings on the Trinity. Calvin, having failed to convert Servetus, became vindictive and saw him as his devoted enemy. On February 13, 1546, Calvin wrote to his friend Farel:

> "If he (Servetus) comes (to Geneva) I shall never let him go out alive if my authority has weight."[15]

For seven years Calvin sought to capture and try Severtus. When Severtus made the mistake of returning to Geneva and attending one of Calvin's services he was recognized and arrested and put on trial. Calvin wrote that he hoped the verdict in Servetus' trial would be the death penalty.[16]

Calvin got his wish and Servetus was convicted of two of the thirty-eight charges brought against him.

He was sentenced to be burned at the stake along with his books, and on October 27, 1553, his sentence was carried out. Outside of Geneva, he was taken to a hill and Nigg records that:

> "A wreath strewn with sulfur was placed on his head. When the faggots were ignited, a piercing cry of horror broke from him. 'Mercy, mercy!' he cried. For more than half an hour the horrible agony continued, for the pyre had been made of half-green wood, which burned slowly. 'Jesus, Son of the eternal God, have mercy on me,' the tormented man cried from the midst of the flames ...."[17]

It should be noted that Servetus was not a citizen of Geneva, but was only visiting the city. Thus, the misdirected piety of John Calvin claimed but another victim.

Nigg said of Calvin,

> "He (Calvin) did not have the faculty for entering into another person's ideas. Rather, he tended to decide arbitrarily that such ideas were diabolically inspired. . . no amount of human or historical broad-mindedness can bring us to excuse Calvin's actions."[18]

This should cause any logical and honest person to question how could this spiritually unsound man be the founder of Protestant Reformed theology. How could Reformed Theology hold him in such high esteem?

Calvin's Inquisition

Calvin, who had denounced Roman Catholicism

for its false beliefs and practices, was giving French refugees asylum from the Inquisition in Geneva. He himself had also been condemned to be burned at the stake absentia, was now conducting his own Reformed Inquisition in Switzerland.

Other Atrocities for which John Calvin was Responsible

The Case of "Freckles" Dunant

In February 1545, a man named "Freckles" Dunant was accused of applying plague venom to the removed foot of a man who was hanged. He was tortured to death in an attempt to make him confess. He died under the torture but would not admit to the crime of spreading the plague. His body was then dragged to the middle of town and burned. This demonstrates the utter lack of compassion or any legal recourse to those who were accused under John Calvin's law. Clearly, Calvin approved and condoned such horrible acts.

On March 7, 1545, Two women were executed by burning at the stake of the crime of spreading the plague. Cottret wrote that

> ". . . Calvin humanely interceded the same day to keep the prisoners from being forced to languish in prison. The Council followed this happy directive and urged the executioner henceforth to "be more diligent in cutting off the hands of malefactors."[19]

Calvin's actions are a testimony to his lack of character and warped sense of compassion.

The Strappado

The executions continued unabated and those who refused to confess were tortured skillfully in a way that would avoid killing them using a strappado. The strappado is a form of torture in which the victim is hung in the air by the wrists with their arms tied behind their back. During this time, two people who were accused sorcerers were decapitated. It was said they composed a plaster of grease and other villainous things that caused people to die. A number of the victims committed suicide to end their torture. One woman who was handcuffed to keep her from taking her life threw herself out of a window to escape the torture. John Calvin not only condoned, but approved of this hideous superstitious torment. Clearly Calvin was ruled by an irrational superstition that has its roots in paganism.

The last execution associated with the plague was on May 16, 1545, in which a total of seven men and twenty-four women were executed. A letter from Calvin attests to 15 of these women being burned at the stake. Calvin's only concern was that the plague had not come to his house.

During this period, a total of thirty-seven people were condemned for spreading the plague. The majority had made confessions, which is not surprising considering the terrible tortures they were made to endure. Calvin also had thirty-four women burned at the stake after accusing them of being witches who caused a plague that had swept through Geneva in 1545.[20]

In 1568, the plague returned and Calvin wrote that fifteen women had already been burned and men were punished more rigorously. Calvin's only concern in all this was that his house had been spared from the plague.[21] On June 23, 1547 several women were accused of dancing which John Calvin forbid. Francoise Favre was the wife of his close friend Ami Perrin who had brought him to Geneva. However, she fell in disfavor with the court because the year earlier she had refused to testify against several of her friends before the Consistory. She again refused to testify and stood up against Calvin. She was thus imprisoned for her actions of defying the Consistory and Calvin.

Calvin Persecuted the Anabaptists

Under Calvin, the Anabaptists were cruelly persecuted. He saw them as his adversaries, mainly because they rejected infant baptism and his unbiblical beliefs and practices. Cottret records:

"Several Anabaptists from the Netherlands were in fact found in Geneva at this time. Among these were Herman de Gerbihan and Benoit d'Anglen, banished during the winter of 1537 with some of their disciples."[22]

The Case of Jacques Gruet

A man named Jacques Gruet, who was a confessed atheist was accused of writing a poster against Calvin accusing him of hypocrisy and hanging it on his pulpit. He was arrested and tortured until he admitted to the crime. He was then executed by beheading on July 26, 1547 because he spoke out against the tyrant of Geneva, John Calvin.

Calvin Was Devoid of Human Kindness

This and many other atrocities were conducted under the direction of John Calvin and clearly show that man was a religious fanatic, a criminal, and a murder. What makes his actions so vile is that he committed these heinous atrocities in the name of Almighty God and under the banner of upholding the truth! These people were not condemned for viable crimes, but because of superstitions, speaking their opinions, or holding beliefs that John Calvin disagreed with. Judging him by his deeds and his warped sense of Christianity, reveals that Calvin was completely devoid of human kindness, and mercy. He certainly had no hint of having the love of Christ in his heart showing no love for his fellow man.

CHAPTER FOUR

UNBIBLICAL BELIEFS AND FAILURES OF JOHN CALVIN

Calvin on the Bible

Calvin on the Bible. In 1536 Calvin wrote:
"The Bible is a knotty, difficult text, whose interpretation demands extensive knowledge. If brought into contact with it unceremoniously, many minds are upset and seized with confusion. The Bible is too old a text in too new a world."[23]

Calvin Believed God Willed That Man Sin

God willed that man sin. Calvin wrote
"God, in a secret and marvellous way, justly wills, the things which men unjustly do." . . . "Although God and the devil will the same thing: they do so in an utterly different manner."[24]

Calvin Taught That All Men are Not to be Saved

God did not will that all men be saved.
". . .that few receive the Gospel; we must fully conclude, that the cause, is the will of God; and that the outward sound of that Gospel strikes the ear in vain, until God is pleased to touch, by it, the heart within."[25]

Calvin concluded that if God wills that all should

be saved then they would be saved. This was the logical conclusion of his idea of predestinated salvation. However, this contradicts God's own word. God says:

> "And the times of this ignorance God winked at; but now commandeth all men every where to repent"   (Acts 17:30)
> "The Lord is not slack concerning his promise, as some men count slackness; but is longsuffering to us-ward, not willing that any should perish, but that all should come to repentance."   (2 Peter 3:9)
> "Who will have all men to be saved, and to come unto the knowledge of the truth." (1 Timothy 2:4)

Calvin Believed God Was the Author of Evil

Calvin believed that God was the author of evil and sin. He said,

> "For, unless there were this good, --that evil things also existed; those evil things would not be permitted, by the Great and Good Omnipotent, to exist at all. For He, without doubt, can as easily refuse to permit to be done what He does not will to be done, as He can do that which He wills to be done. Unless we fully believe this, the very beginning of our faith is perilled: by which, we profess to believe in God ALMIGHTY!"[26]

The conclusion is clear that he believed that God was the author of evil because evil could not have existed unless God allowed it. He believed that God, in allowing evil, caused it.

Calvin Believed in Baptismal Regeneration

Calvin believed in baptismal regeneration. In The Institutes Calvin said,

> "For as God, regenerating us in baptism, ingrafts us into the fellowship of his Church, and makes us his by adoption, so we have said that he performs the office of a provident parent, in continually supplying the food by which he may sustain and preserve us in the life to which he has begotten us by his word."[27]

He further stated,

> ". . . Baptism is, according to Paul, a seal of our future resurrection."[28]

It must also be noted that he taught that baptism was initiatory sign that believers were admitted to the Church. However, he continues and says baptism:

> ". . . is to be a sign and evidence of our purification, or (better to explain my meaning) it is a kind of sealed instrument by which he assures us that all our sins are so deleted, covered, and effaced, that they will never come into his sight, never be mentioned, never imputed."[29]

Note the last part of his statement. Baptism is yes a sign, but it is not a "sealed instrument by he assures us that all our sins are so deleted, covered, and effaced, that they will never come into his sight, never be mentioned, never imputed." This certainly suggests Calvin believed in a form of baptismal regeneration.

Calvin Was a Liar

Calvin was a liar. When Calvin was being severely criticized after the burning of Michael Servetus he sought to defend himself by writing:

> "There was spread abroad, in many places, a rumour, that this vain person (Servetus) was severely bound in prison: whereas, he was perfectly free, and flying about the city openly, every day. And with what malignity some virulent ones imagined and stated, that we wished him to be put to death, you are yourselves our best witnesses."[30]

However, as noted above, long before Servetus came to Geneva and was murdered, Calvin was planning his death.

Calvin Failed as a Pastor

Calvin failed as a pastor. Zweig writes that:

> "In 1543, after the plague struck Geneva, Sebastian Castellio was the only divine in Geneva to visit the sick and console the dying; the Geneva Consistory (made mostly of pastors) and Calvin himself refused to visit the sick, Calvin directed his servants to declare him "indispensable" and being "indispensable" he made no effort to comfort, visit, or minister to the sick. Later when criticized for his actions and writing in his own defense that "it would not do to weaken the whole Church in order to help a part of it."[31]

Clearly, John Calvin thought a great deal of his own

worth. Calvin ignored God's word which explains,
> *"Pure religion and undefiled before God and the Father is this, To visit the fatherless and widows in their affliction, and to keep himself unspotted from the world." (James 1:27)*

Paul instructed believers,
> *"I beseech you therefore, brethren, by the mercies of God, that ye present your bodies a living sacrifice, holy, acceptable unto God, which is your reasonable service." (Romans 12:1)*

Calvin's refusal to help those in his church who were desperately ill seems to indicate a weak faith. His actions appear to show that his faith was not strong enough to believe that God would protect him as he ministered to others in their distress. By not exposing himself to the sick, he deserted his post, being more concerned about his own well-being than the welfare of his flock.

He appears to be more concerned about himself than he his flock he claimed God had sent him to.

Calvin and Excommunication

Calvin believed that "the Church" had the power to excommunicate. Cottret records that:
> "Calvin asked for excommunication without fail of 'fornicators, avaricious people, idolaters, slanderers, and drunkards, devoted to plunder.' In the sixteenth century, far from being simple spiritual acts, the Lord's Supper and its complement, excommunication, were powerful levers for directing public morality."[32]

Calvin and Transubstantiation

To be excommunicated in Geneva meant one would be denied partaking in the Lord's Supper which was paramount from being removed from the protection of the church, the civil government, and the blessings of God. Calvin saw the Lord's Supper as a sacrament. Calvin wrote,

> "We therefore confess with one voice that in receiving the sacrament faithfully according to the ordinance of the Lord we are truly made participants in the very substance of the body and the blood of Jesus Christ."[33]

That clearly is transubstantiation, which is the false doctrine of Roman Catholicism that the elements of the "Eucharist" literally becomes the actual flesh and blood of Jesus Christ and thereby effects forgiveness of sins.

Nowhere does the Bible present the Lord's Supper as a sacrament. There are no sacraments in biblical Christianity that have saving properties or that are necessary for salvation. (Rom. 3:24, 11:6; Eph. 2:8-9; 2 Tim. 1:9; Tit. 3:5) Baptism and the Lord's Supper are simply ordinances of a local assembly that picture symbolically salvation and Christ's atonement. They impart no spiritual benefit other than seeing in them the spiritual truths that they symbolize.

No church can excommunicate or remove the salvation of anyone. A local church can and should practice church discipline for its members who are involved in public sin and who are unrepentant. When applied, the disciplined person loses the fellowship of the congregation which is designed by God to shame them into repentance. A church cannot give salvation, and therefore a church cannot take it away, as salvation is solely the work of God. However, a local church can remove from their fellowship a member, who by his unrepentant sin, brings disgrace on the whole congregation.

The Selfishness of Calvin

Calvin's deeds show him to be an uncaring and uncompassionate man not showing the love of Christ that comes with true salvation. One can get some insight into John Calvin's capacity toward love and human compassion in his statement to Farel while he was in Strasburg, Germany in May 1539. Calvin was unmarried and stated his desires toward acquiring a wife saying,

> "Remember well what I seek for in her. I am not of the insane race of those lovers who, once taken by a woman's beauty, cherish even her faults. The only beauty that seduces me is that of a woman who is chaste, considerate, modest, economical, patient; who I can hope, finally, will be attentive to my health."[34]

It is hard to miss the selfishness in his thoughts of the qualifications of one who he would accept as a wife. In 1540, while in Strasburg, Calvin was married to Idelette de Bure, a widow with two children. Writing about their short honeymoon Calvin said,

> "In truth, out of fear that our marriage would be too happy, the Lord from the beginning moderated our joy." He further explained that one must know

"how to keep one's countenance."[35]

Calvin's True Belief About Marriage

Due to a plague in the city Idelette moved to the country. Calvin was prompted to write in her absence,

> "My wife is in my thoughts day and night, deprived of counsel because she is deprived of her master."[36]

CHAPTER FIVE

THE TENANTS OF CALVINISM

The Groups in Calvinism

The beliefs and teachings of John Calvin became the distinguishing characteristics of the Protestant Reformed churches and some Baptists. Calvinists are divided into several groups: the extremist, are called "Hyper" or "Five Point" Calvinists, and the "Moderate Calvinists."

The Hyper-Calvinists and TULIP

The Hyper and Five Point Calvinists hold to the five points of Calvinism, which are stated in the acrostic TULIP.

The Moderate Calvinist

The Moderate Calvinist may accept one or more of these five points, but not all. The Hyper or Five Point Calvinistic teaching of "Limited Atonement" is generally rejected by the Moderate Calvinist. Simply stated, the heart of Calvinistic theology is the view that claims that God predestined or elected some to be saved and others to be lost. Those elected to salvation are decreed by God to receive salvation and cannot "resist God's grace." However, those that God elected to be lost are born condemned eternally to the Lake of Fire, and He will not allow them be saved. The five points of Calvinism spring from this false understanding of election and predestination.

This controversy began during the Reformation

in the 16th Century and grew out of Calvin's teaching. According to Calvinism, those that God, in His sovereignty, has chosen to be saved, will be saved by God's "irresistible grace." The man "elected" by God to salvation cannot reject salvation. The rest of humanity, not chosen by God to receive everlasting life, has no opportunity to be saved. According to the Hyper Calvinist, God in the past has decreed their damnation. Today this theology is found in what is called "Covenant" or "Reformed" theology. This is taught by Presbyterians, Reformed churches and some Baptists.

A Biblical Look at the Five Points of Calvinism (TULIP)

This teaching is referred to as "Five Point Calvinism." The five points are represented by using the acrostic "TULIP."

T - Total depravity of man.
U - Unconditional election.
L - Limited atonement.
I - Irresistible grace.
P - Perseverance of the saints.

TOTAL DEPRAVITY

The first article of Calvinism deals with man as a sinner and teaches that a man is "totally depraved," unable, having no ability to receive salvation. The Bible clearly teaches that man is born in a spiritually corrupt state that affects his mind, intelligence, emotion, and will. The Bible calls this state "unrighteousness" which means not being right with God. When Adam sinned, he brought into the world both spiritual and physical death and passed his sinful nature to all his progeny. Ephesians 2:1 states man in his natural unregenerated state is indeed ". . .dead in trespasses and sins." On this truth, biblical Christians certainly agree. However, the Scriptures do not use the words "total depravity" nor teach this concept in the sense that the Calvinist does. Depravity means to be corrupt, debase, impaired, perverted, etc. The Calvinist goes to the extreme by applying this word to man's sinful condition and concludes that man's free will has no part in his coming to Christ and receiving salvation.

The Scriptures clearly teach that man apart from God's intervention, cannot savingly come to Christ. Romans 3:10-18 describe all men as being unrighteous and as verse 10 states:

"As it is written, There is none righteous, no, not one." (Romans 3:10)

Man in his fallen state does not understand or seek God, and there is no fear of God before their eyes. God says,

"For all have sinned, and come short of the glory of God" (Romans 3:23)

and that man's righteousness is as "filthy rags" (Isa. 64:6).

Paul revealed the state of the carnal mind:

"Because the carnal mind is enmity against God: for it is not subject to the law of God, neither indeed can be. So then they that are in the flesh cannot please God." (Romans 8:7-8)

But that does not mean that a man cannot with God's intervention believe and be saved.

Certainly, salvation cannot be merited or earned

as Ephesians 2:8-9 teaches,

> *"For by grace are ye saved through faith;*
> *and that not of yourselves: it is the gift of*
> *God: Not of works, lest any man should*
> *boast." (Ephesians 2:8-9)*

Therefore, a man cannot "will" himself to be saved because in his natural state he has no righteousness nor seeks God. Jesus explained that,

> *"No man can come to me, except the*
> *Father which hath sent me draw him: and*
> *I will raise him up at the last day." (John*
> *6:44)*

Jesus' words reveal how an unrighteous man can be saved and receive salvation by faith. It is God the Father who draws the sinner to salvation.

This is the principle that Calvinism confuses and carries to the extreme. God's word explains that after Adam and Eve sinned, they knew good from evil.

> *"And the LORD God said, Behold, the*
> *man is become as one of us, to know*
> *good and evil: and now, lest he put forth*
> *his hand, and take also of the tree of life,*
> *and eat, and live for ever" (Genesis*
> *3:22)*

What the Calvinist does not accept or understand is that man can respond to God, using his will, to accept salvation when convicted by the Holy Spirit. Without the intervention of the Holy Spirit, a person does not seek God or desire to receive God's forgiveness. However, when the Holy Spirit illuminates the man's mind and reveals his lost state, God also gives that man the ability to respond with his will and be saved. The same man can also reject God's offer of salvation, and God will allow him to do so not forcing a man to accept what he does not want.

Carrying man's lost condition to the extreme, the Calvinist teaches that God, exercising His sovereignty, first elected and then decreed certain individuals to salvation in time past. According to them, Christ's death was not for all people as 1 John 2:2 states,

> *"And he is the propitiation (full payment) for our sins: and not for ours only, but also for the sins of the whole world." (1 John 2:2)*

In order to support   their theology they conclude that Jesus only died for the few whom He chose to save. This belief directly contradicts the clear statement of 1 John 2:2. God then, according to Reformed Theology, extended "irresistible" grace to those whom He elected, meaning that God save these people without any action on their part. In other words, God forced them to be saved. Following their baseless logic therefore, a man has nothing to do with his receiving salvation because God chooses to save him and make him believe. In other words,

> "Election is God's choice for some persons."[37]

This logically means that God does not elect to save anyone else but His few chosen "elect."   Even though the Scripture repeatedly, in presenting the Gospel, proclaims that a man must believe in order to be saved, the Calvinist teaches that only those whom God has predestined to be saved can believe and only when God supernaturally causes them to believe.

UNCONDITIONAL ELECTION

The concept of unconditional election purports that God predestined who He would save and who He would not allow to be saved by withholding His grace, thus condemning them to the Lake of Fire. Biblical Christians have strong objections to this tenant of Calvinism. The reason is that unconditional election means that God chose to save some and not to save others. Those who reject Calvinism contend that this belief is an attack on God's very character and nature. This belief contradicts the biblical teaching that Jesus Christ died and paid the sin debt of all men (1 John 2:2); and that God ". . . will have all men to be saved" (1 Tim. 2:4); and that God's nature is love, which means seeking the best for all men (1 John 4:7-8, 16). These Scriptures and others refute the idea that God chooses to give life to most of mankind and gives them life in order to send them to hell. No-where in the Word of God does He say that He decreed who would be saved and who would not be saved. Men are saved based on their acceptance or rejection of God's gift of grace which He offers to all men. Romans 1:18-23 plainly teaches that man is condemned because he refuses to believe God and accept God's grace. Jesus clearly stated

"And this is the condemnation, that light is come into the world, and men loved darkness rather than light, because their deeds were evil. For every one that doeth evil hateth the light, neither cometh to the light, lest his deeds should be reproved." *(John 3:19-20)*

The light without question is Jesus Christ and the

Gospel. Jesus said that men choose to reject the "light" because their deeds are evil, and they refuse to come to the "light" because the "light" reproves their sin. The basis of man's condemnation is not God, but the man himself who knows the truth and refuses to believe and submit himself to his Creator and Savior. Proverbs 1:29 tells us,

> *"For that they hated knowledge, and did not choose the fear of the LORD" (Proverbs 1:29)*

Those who hated the knowledge of God chose not to believe and fear God and thus they condemned themselves; God has always offered grace and mercy to all who will accept it.

LIMITED ATONEMENT

Limited atonement is another natural false assumption of the Calvinist. Calvinists assume that if only those who God has predestined to be saved will be saved, then God limits atonement to only those He elects. All men therefore cannot be saved because God's grace is offered only to those who He has chosen. This is a teaching based on human logic and not on God's word.

1 Peter 1:2 explains who are the elect.

> *"Elect according to the foreknowledge of God the Father, through sanctification of the Spirit, unto obedience and sprinkling of the blood of Jesus Christ: Grace unto you, and peace, be multiplied." (1 Peter 1:2)*

God says He elects according to His "foreknowledge" meaning His knowing in the future. God is omniscient and knows all things past, present, and future. He knew who would believe, and thus He elected what salvation would be provided for those who believed. The election was not for who would be saved, but what salvation would provide to those who accepted His grace. More will be said about this later.

IRRESISTIBLE GRACE

Being true to their human reasoning, the Calvinists conclude that grace then must be irresistible. If God is sovereign and forces a man to be saved, then the man cannot resist. Those to whom God elected to save will be saved a part from any action on their part. Thus, a man whom God has elected cannot resist God's grace and will be saved. God says,

> *"For this is good and acceptable in the sight of God our Saviour; Who will have all men to be saved, and to come unto the knowledge of the truth."* *(1 Timothy 2:3-4)*

The Scriptures declare that God's very nature is to love. God's love is not conditional on a person meriting or deserving His love. No one deserves God's mercy and grace. But God offers His love unconditionally to all who will believe. God says clearly His desire is that all men come to the knowledge of the truth. This precludes there being anyone whom God has excluded from His offer of grace. God wants everyone to be saved. If grace is irresistible, as the Calvinist teaches, then why does He not, as a loving God and Creator, save everyone? The answer is plain that most men do not want to believe and they prevent God from giving them His free gift of salvation because they love their sin more than their souls.

PERSEVERANCE OF THE SAINTS

The Calvinists continue in using human reasoning to confuse the doctrine of the security and assurance of salvation. They change the words the Bible uses of "assurance" and teach "the perseverance of the saints." (See 1 Thess. 1:5; Heb. 6:11, 10:22) Calvinism correctly teaches that once saved, a person cannot lose their salvation. However, the term "perseverance of the saints" by definition presents a false understanding of the "security of the believer." Their word "perseverance" means to "continue on a course of action" or refers to steadfastness. Their word implies that God will not allow a believer to "backslide" or fall into sin. This may seem to be a minor point to differentiate between "perseverance" and "security," but the words have different meanings. A believer can and will sin, and can sin to the point that God will chasten him and even take the believers life if he will not repent. (See 1 John 1:8-10) The believer is assured that he is "secure" in Christ and will go to heaven. Once saved, a person cannot be lost because he did nothing to earn his salvation and cannot do anything to keep it or lose it. (See Rom. 3:20, 27-28, 4:2, 8:38-39; 9:11, 11:6; 1 Cor. 1:29-31; Eph. 2:8-9; 2 Tim. 1:9; Tit. 3:3-5) Biblically, salvation is totally the work of God and once saved a person is kept secure by the power of God unto salvation.

God said:

> "Blessed be the God and Father of our Lord Jesus Christ, which according to his abundant mercy hath begotten us again

unto a lively hope by the resurrection of Jesus Christ from the dead, To an inheritance incorruptible, and undefiled, and that fadeth not away, reserved in heaven for you, Who are kept by the power of God through faith unto salvation ready to be revealed in the last time" (1 Peter 1:3-5).

The Bible clearly teaches that a man can "backslide" and can allow sin to rule his life. Hebrews 12:6-11, 1 Corinthians 11:32, and 1 John 5:16 teach that God will chasten an unrepentant, sinning believer even unto death to end his rebellion. The Biblical doctrine is the "security" not the "perseverance" of the saints. A saint of God can fail God, but God will not fail the saint. God gives eternal life to those who by faith repent and receive His free gift of salvation. Once saved the believer cannot be lost because God has forgiven all their past, present, and future sins. Thus, a true believer is secure in God's grace. When a man receives Christ he becomes a new creature, a saved child of God and is indwelt by the spirit of God. He cannot be lost once saved. (See 2 Cor. 5:17) When the unrepentant believer dies he will in eternity be judged but not to condemnation. Christ's judgment of believers is for reward, not condemnation. Thus, the unrepentant sinner who dies will receive no reward as 1 Corinthians 3:14-15 states.

"If any man's work abide which he hath built thereupon, he shall receive a reward. If any man's work shall be burned, he shall suffer loss: but he himself shall be saved; yet so as by fire."

(1 Corinthians 3:14-15)

None of the tenants of TULIP meet the biblical test and they present a false view of the doctrines of election, God's grace, and of salvation.

CHAPTER SIX

SOME FAMOUS PREACHERS OF THE PAST WHO WERE CALVINISTS

Charles Spurgeon

Charles Spurgeon, one of the greatest preachers in recent times, dealt with the matter by alternately preaching both salvation by grace and man's responsibility to respond to God's offer of redemption. He compromised God's word by preaching the Calvinist doctrine of election to salvation one Sunday (Calvinism), and the next Sunday preaching that man must exercise his will and believe on the Lord Jesus Christ. Like most Calvinists, he made the error of seeing election as referring to a person being chosen for salvation. He seems not to have seen that biblically election refers to God's plan for how God's elected plan would benefit the believer. The Calvinist takes great stock in asserting that Charles Spurgeon was a Calvinist Many Baptists use Spurgeon to justify their being Calvinists. Paul warned

> ". . .God forbid: yea, let God be true, but every man a liar; as it is written, That thou mightest be justified in thy sayings, and mightest overcome when thou art judged." (Romans 3:4)

Arthur Pink

Others, such as the famous writer Arthur Pink, along with most of those of the Five Point Calvinist persuasion, boldly taught that God has predestined some to be saved, and equally predestined others to be damned to hell. The one predestined to salvation will absolutely be saved and there is nothing he can do to prevent it. This is their teaching of "Irresistible Grace." They conclude that if God offers grace then it cannot be refused because God is sovereign in all He does. The result of their false logic and theology is that they conclude the poor unfortunate soul who has not been chosen by God and who is not offered grace, but is born for hell and cannot receive Christ.

What is interesting and also tragic is that Pink, who is hailed as a great theologian, does not see the error in his teaching. For example he quotes Isaiah 59:2 in his book *"Gleanings in Genesis."*

> *"But your iniquities have separated between you and your God, and your sins have hid his face from you, that he will not hear. (Isaiah 59:1-2)*

Yet, he misses what God says in verse 1,

> *"Behold, the LORD'S hand is not shortened, that it cannot save; neither his ear heavy, that it cannot hear."*

The verse says it is the iniquities of the sinner that separate him from God and are the cause of God's "hiding" His face and not hearing the sinner. Calvinism contradicts God's word and proclaims it is God's sovereign choice and action to hide is face and not hear the sinner. As one reads the contents of the Reformers in their vast numbers of their writings, this serious error is made continually.

Popular Modern Day Radio Preachers Who Are Calvinists

John MacArthur

John MacArthur, of the radio program "Grace to You", is typical of most Five Point Calvinists. He states that the dispute over this matter exists only because man does not want to accept God's sovereignty. Furthermore, he proclaims that the truth of God's sovereignty offends man's pride and offends his sense of fairness. MacArthur resorts to name calling and quotes Arthur Pink, in calling those who reject Calvinism as being "merit-mongers." He further states that some men reject the sovereignty of God in salvation:

> ". . . because fallen man wants to assume some responsibility--even if it is a very little--for having believed. He desperately wants some credit for having made the right choice."[38]

MacArthur makes a straw man of the non-Calvinists of his own imagination and attacks it.

There is no more absolute truth than the fact that no biblical student or preacher of the Bible would deny God's complete sovereignty over all things. Nor would any true believer, who knows anything about the Bible and salvation, teach that salvation is earned and thereby be a "merit monger." That is a foolish, childish, rude, uncalled for, unscholarly, and untruthful statement.

The Bible is emphatically clear that man cannot merit or work for his salvation as it is the work of God.

But the Calvinist mistakenly infers that if a man uses his will and believes in Jesus Christ, it means man is earning or meriting his salvation. In other words, if a man uses his will to believe and accept God's free gift of salvation he is earning his salvation. That is an unacceptable conclusion to those who believe God's word. The one who believes God's word will reject the tenants of Calvinism for the reason that it is not biblical and contradicts God's word. Salvation, as Ephesians 2:8-9 state, is God's gift free gift of grace. A gift is not something merited or earned, and it can be accepted or rejected. If a person receives a gift it is illogical to assume that the gift was earned or merited because that is not the character of a gift.

MacArthur further says that man is repulsed by the doctrine of election because it seems unfair that God would choose to save some, but not others. He is correct. He concludes,

> ". . . the reason man so strongly wants to have a part in his own salvation is because he wants to exercise his pride."[39]

MacArthur should not make emphatic and uninformed statements about what is in people's hearts. This is the kind of judging that Jesus condemned when He said,

> "Judge not, that ye be not judged."
> (Matthew 7:1)

It is a serious error of MacArthur, to judge the hearts of men he does not know. Furthermore, it is tragic that a man of his popularity would equate accepting Calvinism to the status of believing God's word, but that is what he does. According to John MacArthur, if you reject Calvinism, you are not a

Bible believer!

Frankly, there are many believers who do not fit into either of MacArthur's supposed categories and they reject the Calvinistic view based solely on what the Bible says about the matter. These people, as does the author of this article, reject both the Calvinistic and Arminian views and appeal to the Scriptures alone. There is compelling biblical evidence to reject both ideas as being unbiblical. There are many godly people who totally accept the sovereignty of God and reject human pride or any participation of man in meriting salvation.

David Jeremiah

After listening to David Jeremiah, of the program "Turning Point" several years ago, when he taught a one week series on election, I wrote him a letter in which I pointed out several inconsistencies of Calvinism with the Bible. He had one of his assistants, Gene Huntsman, reply to my letter. In the letter Huntsman stated,

> "In the study of predestination and election our poor minds may not reconcile them both, but our faith knows them both and holds them both to be truth. Scripture is addressed to faith not reason."[40]

Clearly, Huntsman does not seem to understand that God's word is absolutely reasonable in all it says. He further quoted some source and stated,

> "Now do not seek to mix these two things (predestination and election) and still more emphatically . . . do not try to 'reconcile them. Profitless controversy

and partisan feeling will be the only result. Who told us to 'reconcile' in our little minds, these seemingly contradictory things? . . . if you undertake to 'reconcile' God's sovereign election with His free offer of salvation to all, you must sacrifice one truth for another."[41]

In other words, he purports the Christian is to blindly accept the Calvinists ideas without question and with no biblical examination. Is this what God's word teaches?

"Study to shew thyself approved unto God, a workman that needeth not to be ashamed, rightly dividing the word of truth" (2 Timothy 2:15)?

He further concludes in this area the truth cannot be understood and it is "profitless" to pursue.

In this reply, David Jeremiah's representative also built a straw man in his poor attempt to defend this unbiblical teaching. His statement that "Scripture is addressed to faith not reason" is grossly unsound. Yes, we do live by faith, but biblical faith is not existential. It is not a "leap into the dark." True faith is based solely in God's revealed word! Our faith is not blind, but its rests on the stated promises and truths of God's inspired word. God is certainly not the author of confusion and further He cannot lie, or contradict Himself. It is a contradiction for God on one hand to state,

"For this is good and acceptable in the sight of God our Saviour; Who will have all men to be saved, and to come unto the knowledge of the truth." (1 Timothy 2:4),

58

and on the other hand decree, as David Jeremiah does and as the Calvinists teach, that some men are elected and born to be condemned to hell.

The reason the Calvinist wishes to condemn those who disagree with them for trying to "reconcile" the matter is because Calvinism is in direct opposition to what God has plainly stated and cannot be biblically defended. They correctly state that they cannot 'reconcile' God decreeing to save some and refusing His grace to others. This is true because you cannot "reconcile" truth with error. You cannot reconcile God being a loving and just God, and on the other hand teach that He withholds His mercy and grace and condemns most of the world to hell, not allowing some people to believe and be saved. This is an unreasonable idea that God's word does not substantiate. There is not one verse in the Bible that states that God has limited His grace or decreed that some men will go to hell without any chance of being saved. Not one verse in the Bible teaches "irresistible grace." Calvinism and Reformed Theology is a false teaching formed in the minds of men who dogmatically support an indefensible system with a flawed theology. Sadly, and tragically the Calvinist dogmatically holds to his view regardless of whether it contradicts God's word or not.

Other well-known modern radio and television Calvinists include the following:

R. C. Sproul, Jr.

R. C. Sproul, Jr. is an American Calvinist theologian, philosopher, author, and pastor and the founder and chairman of Ligonier Ministries who has the daily radio program "Renewing Your Mind."

Mark Driscoll

Mark Driscoll, is the popular pastor and founder of Mars Hill Church in Seattle.

John Piper

John Piper, a Calvinistic Baptist preacher and author currently serving as the Pastor for Preaching and Vision of Bethlehem Baptist Church in Minneapolis, Minnesota.

R. Albert Mohler

R. Albert Mohler, Jr. is an American theologian and the ninth president of Southern Baptist Theological Seminary in Louisville, Kentucky.

Charles Joseph Mahaney

Charles Joseph Mahaney is the president of Sovereign Grace Ministries, and one of the founding pastors and leaders of Covenant Life Church.

CHAPTER SEVEN

DOCTRINAL PROBLEMS WITH CALVINISM

Calvinism Destroys God's Grace and Love

Calvinism is contrary to God's grace itself, which stems from God's love and unmerited favor toward man. To accept Calvinism is to proclaim that God does not love all His creation, and that nullifies His grace. God's grace is the action of His love. Calvinism will agree that God is love, but it in reality portrays God as unloving and unjust to most men on earth. Calvinism restricts God's love to only a part of His creation, which makes a lie out of God's statements that He loves the world (John 3:16; Rom. 5:8; 1 Joh. 4:9-10). ". . . God is love." (1 John 4:8) God reveals to us that He is love and that is His very nature, therefore He cannot go against who He is and deny His love to some because He chooses not to love them. God says He is love and He cannot go against His nature. God's sovereignty does not allow Him to deny who He is.

How then can the Calvinist accept that God is love, when they believe He withholds his grace from most of the world? Not one word in the Bible limits God's love. God's love is offered freely, and is only limited by sinful men who will not accept His love. However, that is not God's fault, but man's. John 3:15-16 states plainly:

> *"God so loved the world, that he gave His*
> *only begotten Son."*

If one truly believes that statement of God's word, then one cannot be a Calvinist. Man goes to hell because he refuses to believe God and as a sinner rejects God. He is not condemned because God decreed him to burn in the Lake of Fire. He is not doomed because God does not to allow the man to repent (Joh. 3:19-20; Rom. 1:18-23).

It is a perversion of God's sovereignty and His grace to conclude that He would violate His own nature and withhold His love from the world. God is just, and therefore His justice demands that if a man rejects His grace, and Christ's payment for his sins, then the man must pay the debt himself. Yet, 1 John 2:2 says clearly that "And he is the propitiation for our sins: and not for ours only, but also for the sins of the whole world." (1 John 2:2)

The question is simply this: "Does God love the world and did Jesus Christ, God incarnate in the flesh, come to the earth, suffer, and die for the sins of mankind?" The biblical answer is overwhelmingly YES! Then how can the Calvinist teach that He did not? On what biblical basis does the Calvinist teach that God did not extend His love to all men, even though they reject that love? God says,

> *"But God commendeth his love toward*
> *us, in that, while we were yet sinners,*
> *Christ died for us."* (Romans 5:8)

There is nothing in the context of this statement that limits God's grace. Paul explains,

> *"Therefore as by the offence of one*
> *(Adam) judgment came upon all men to*
> *condemnation; even so by the*

righteousness of one (Jesus Christ) the
free gift came upon all men unto
justification of life." (Romans 5:18)

The Free Gift

In other words, all men stand condemned by their sins, but Jesus Christ offers the free "gift" of "justification of life" to "all" men. Verse 19 says, "For as by one man's disobedience many were made sinners, so by the obedience of one shall many be made righteous." (Romans 5:19) The verse says that many will be made righteous, and clearly that limits those who will be saved. However, those made righteous are those who by faith believed and accept Jesus Christ as their Salvation. Christ died and paid the sin debt for all men, but only those who accept His free gift will receive His righteousness and resulting salvation.

Calvinism has a False View of Man's Will

The Calvinist contends that using one's will to receive salvation is a work and man thus takes part in his receiving his salvation. As the Bible clearly teaches a man cannot merit or earn his salvation. However, the Calvinists pervert this simple truth and attempt to make this truth fit their theology, concluding that a man's will has no function in his being saved. (See Eph. 2:8-9) The question is "Does willfully believing and accepting Jesus Christ as one's Savior constitute a "work?"

One of the first arguments the Calvinists use to support their belief is that a man is totally depraved, which means his will is also depraved, and cannot willfully believe and be saved. As pointed out earlier, the Bible does not use the word "depraved" but rather says that he is "unrighteous."

Using the Word "Depravity"

Using the word "depravity" limits a person's respond under any circumstances. They conclude that God in the past decreed who He would save and then at some point in time in that "elected" person's life God gives him irresistible grace and the person is saved. They reason correctly that man is dead in his trespasses and sin and so being spiritually dead, he can do anything to save himself. Yet, they take the extreme and unbiblical position that man cannot believe unless God forces that belief on him. Their idea is that man's will has no part in a person believing and accepting Jesus Christ as his Savior. They conclude God decreed the person would be saved and then God thrusts salvation on the person regardless of the person's will. Furthermore, their argument is that if a man chooses to be saved, his act of using his will is a form of work, and works cannot save.

Man Has a Choice

Truly, works cannot save, but does that mean that a man, who hears God's word and is convicted by the Holy Spirit of his sins, cannot then accept by faith God's offer of redemption? If God offers salvation, as so many scriptures teach, why cannot a man accept His grace? Does a person responding to the convicting power of the Holy Spirit constitute a work?

Examples From the Bible

The Bible gives us examples of those to whom God offered choices. God did not force His will upon them, but offered them a proposition to which they could respond. They, in turn, had to use their wills to accept or reject God's proposal.

Adam and Eve

In Genesis 2:16-17 God said to Adam,
> *"And the LORD God commanded the man, saying, Of every tree of the garden thou mayest freely eat: But of the tree of the knowledge of good and evil, thou shalt not eat of it: for in the day that thou eatest thereof thou shalt surely die."* (Genesis 2:16-17)

Did not God give Adam and Eve a choice? He was warned that if he ate fruit from the forbidden tree he would surely die. Thus, how Adam used his will had consequences. God gave Adam a clear choice. Eat of all the other trees, but not this one. The Lord allowed Adam to use his will. Did Adam and Eve use their wills in making their fateful decision? The Calvinist cannot deny this plain truth, but he then distorts Adam using his will in response to God by concluding that after Adam sinned, God took away man's ability to use his will. Yes, man's will was made corrupt in the Fall, but it was not removed nor was it beyond God's ability to have the Holy Spirit illuminate so the man could respond to God's drawing him and believe as John 6:44 states.

65

Abel and Cain

In Genesis 4, Abel and Cain were also given a choice. This was clearly after the Fall , a minor detail that John Calvin and his followers ignore. Both of Adam's sons could have obeyed God and by faith presented to Him a blood sacrifice and be accepted, or they could reject God's word, disobey God and be rejected by Him. Abel made the correct choice and Cain did not. It should be noted what God said to Cain in Genesis 4:7,

> *"If thou doest well, shalt thou not be*
> *accepted? and if thou doest not well, sin*
> *lieth at the door. And unto thee shall be*
> *his desire, and thou shalt rule over him."*

In other words, God says that if Cain had believed God and by faith offered a proper sacrifice would he not have been accepted?   God gave Cain a choice and because he did not believe and fear God, he willingly rejected God, fully knowing the truth and what he was doing.   He rejected God's offer of grace and stood condemned.

Throughout the whole of the Bible, God gave men choices. He always told them what was righteous, meaning what was "right" and was His will. He also warned them of making the wrong choice. Why does God do this if men are predestined by God as to what they will do, and have no ability to do otherwise? God also gave the children of Israel a choice in the offering of an animal as a symbolic burnt offering for their sins. The burnt offering did not take away sin, but is a picture of Christ's later suffering, shedding His blood and dying for the sins of the world. Leviticus 1:2 plainly states that giving the burnt offering was not a commandment, but it was to be a free will offering of the people in repentance of their sins. The Hebrews were not obligated to offer a burnt sacrifice for their sins. Yet, if they believed God, they would obey Him, confess their sins, and want to honor the Lord in their offering of a sacrifice.

The Children of Israel

It is very important to note the wording of God's instructions to Moses.

> "Speak unto the children of Israel, and say unto them, If any man of you bring an offering unto the LORD, ye shall bring your offering of the cattle, even of the herd, and of the flock. If his offering be a burnt sacrifice of the herd, let him offer a male without blemish: he shall offer it of his own voluntary will at the door of the tabernacle of the congregation before the LORD." (Leviticus 1:2-3)

The Calvinists claim that God only offers His grace to those He has selected and the rest of mankind is doomed, by God's will and degree to the fires of hell. Yet, in His instructions concerning the offering of a sin offering by the children of Israel, God made no restriction. He said "If any man of you bring an offering to the Lord." God also said in the New Testament,

> "And it shall come to pass, that whosoever shall call on the name of the Lord shall be saved." (Acts 2:21) (See Romans 10:13).

Never in God's word is there even a hint that God

withholds His grace from anyone who desires to come. Nowhere in God's word does it say that God choose to offer His grace to some and withhold it from others. When God reveals the truth to a person it simply means that God understands that the person can respond. That is why Christians preach and teach the Gospel. Through the preaching and teaching, God is revealing Himself to sinners and showing them, through the convicting power of the Holy Spirit how they can be saved. Hebrews 11 abounds with men and women who obeyed when God. When God told them His will, they obeyed, believed God, and it was "counted unto them for righteous." These hosts of the "heroes of faith" used their God given wills to honor God. They used their wills through the power and ability God gave them. Their faith did not come from themselves, but came from God. They did not act in their own righteousness, but in the righteousness and power of God.

Joshua beckoned Israel to serve the Lord saying,

> "And if it seem evil unto you to serve the LORD, choose you this day whom ye will serve; whether the gods which your fathers served that were on the other side of the flood, or the gods of the Amorites, in whose land ye dwell: but as for me and my house, we will serve the LORD." (Joshua 24:15)

Israel had a choice to serve God or idols. This was a choice of salvation or damnation. Joshua warned them

> "If ye forsake the LORD, and serve strange gods, then he will turn and do

68

you hurt, and consume you, after that he
hath done you good." (Joshua 24:20)

If they were totally depraved and could not respond then why did God speak to them through Joshua and offer them the choice? If all were "predestined to heaven or hell with no ability to respond except according to how God had programmed them, why offer the choice? If any of the children of Israel, who heard Joshua's promise of salvation, were not permitted by God to respond, then the choice and the offer would have been a lie to those poor souls. God's offer of grace was God enabling man to respond. If God offers He cannot deny what He offers. If you take away man's ability to use his God given will to obey God then you also take away his responsibility for his actions.

Plainly, God gave them a choice, and they used their God given wills to accept or reject God's offer. The Calvinist has no biblical basis to say that a man's will has no part in his salvation. Over sixty times in the New Testament God tells man to believe and be saved. Belief is an act of one's will. However, God is clear that a lost man cannot on His own be saved. It is true that a man cannot by himself will himself to be saved. Yet, when God draws a man, then man's will is illuminated and he is enabled by the Holy Spirit, he can through God's power and provision, believe and accept by faith God's offer of grace. Surely, a man cannot do this on his own. It is false doctrine to deny this vital and necessary act of God, the Holy Spirit, beckoning a person to be saved, by offering man salvation. God does not force a man to believe and accept His grace and use man as a robot. He illuminates a man's will, shows him the truth, and offers Him forgiveness of sins and eternal life.

Inconsistencies of Calvinism

There are many inconsistencies in Reformed Theology. God says in Hebrews 11:6,

"But without faith it is impossible to please him: for he that cometh to God must believe that he is, and that he is a rewarder of them that diligently seek him."

Several truths stand out sharply in this passage. Plainly, the heart of God's plan is that without faith in God, it is impossible for a man to please or come to God. The man who comes to God must believe that God is. This means that God exists, is man's Creator, and that every man is responsible to Him. A "depraved" robot, which is the Calvinist's view of man, cannot express faith, nor believe or seek God. The Calvinist's irresistible grace means preprogrammed grace!? Furthermore, God says that faith is inseparably tied to "diligently seeking Him." A robot cannot seek anything, but can only can perform the programming he is given. How can a "totally depraved" man desire to seek something he is incapable of knowing exists? The context of God's statement is of the saving faith, of men who heard God's promises, and by faith, received them. By God's very definition of faith Calvinism is refuted. Calvinism is a maze of inconsistencies and unbiblical conclusions that defy any logic and have no support from God's word. There are no inconsistencies with God as He is a God of order, organization, and true logic.

The Misuse of Words by the Calvinists Pas (Whosoever, All)

"Whosoever" - "pas" - The word "pas" (whosoever) in John 3:16, Acts 2:21, presents a problem for the Calvinist because the word means "whoever" and "whatever person: no matter who," and in the verse it means "whoever believes."[42] The Calvinist twists the word to infer it means "all the believing ones of those who were predestinated to believe by God, in contrast to the ones God will not allow to be saved because He withholds His grace from them." However this is not substantiated by the Greek definitions of the words used, or by teachings of the New Testament.

> *"And it shall come to pass, that whosoever shall call on the name of the Lord shall be saved." (Acts 2:21)*

In Acts 2:21, Robertson identifies the phrase "shall call on" as:

> "First aorist middle subjunctive of epikaleo, common verb, to call to, middle voice for oneself in need. Indefinite relative clause with ean and so subjunctive, puncticular idea, in any single case, and so aorist."[43]

It can accurately be translated as "whatever person would call on the Lord will be saved." In other words, whatever person would call on the name of the Lord "sozo" (shall be saved), meaning shall be delivered.

In John 3:15-16, the word "pas" as a pronoun modifies the word believes. The verse literally says,

> *"For God so loved the world, that he gave*

his only begotten Son, that whosoever (whatever person or whoever) believeth in him should not perish, but have everlasting life." (John 3:16)

The Greek dictionary by Arndt-Gingrich says this in the context John 3:15-16 it means "everyone who, whoever."[44]

The Greek word(s) "pas, pasa, pan, ras, rasa, ran," are used in the New Testament and translated hundreds of times "all, whosoever, everyone, whole, all manner, etc." The word "pas" is used 99 times in the New Testament. The word is all inclusive and how it is modified determines who it is referring to. In John 3:15-16 and Acts 2:21 the word "whosoever" simply means every person who believes will be saved. The word "whosoever" is not restricted to the supposed few who are decreed to receive irresistible grace from God but to all the world.

Kosmos (World)

"World" - kosmos. - The Calvinist insists that the word "world" used in verses such as John 3:16, and 1 John 2:2 does not mean the whole world, but only applies to the elected few who are decreed by God to receive irresistible grace. Note how explicit is 1 John 2:2,

"And he is the propitiation for our sins: and not for ours only, but also for the sins of the whole (holos "all") world (kosmos)."

The word when used with the article refers to the whole of something. For example:

"And when he had found him, he brought him unto Antioch. And it came to pass,

> *that a whole year they assembled*
> *themselves with the church, and taught*
> *much people. . ." (Acts 11:26)*

Barnabas and Saul taught at Antioch for one year. If the Calvinist was consistent he would have to translate the verse to mean they assembled for some indefinite or unspecified period of time. However, the use of the modifier "whole" restricts the phrase to mean one complete year.

Further, the word "world" is kosmos and denotes as Arndt-Gingrich states,

> ". . . in philosophy usage the world as the
> sum total of everything here, and now. . .
> 3. as the sum total of all beings above the
> level of the animals. . . 4. the world as the
> earth, the planet on which we live. . . b.
> the as the habitation of mankind. . . .c.
> the world in contrast to heaven, . . . 5. the
> world as all mankind, . . b. of all mankind,
> but especially believers. 8. totality, sum
> total."[45]

Note the use of "whole world" in 1 John 5:19:

> *"And we know that we are of God, and*
> *the whole world lieth in wickedness."*

The Calvinist interpretation contradicts the statement of the passage 1 John 2:2. John makes the unmistakable distinction between the whole world and those who are identified as believers. It is a gross misrepresentation of this phrase to limit it to any individuals elected by God through His supposed irresistible grace.

These passages state that Jesus Christ was the full payment, the "propitiation, " for the believer's sins, and also for all mankind. Jesus' suffering and payment for sins was for all of mankind. Sadly, only those who by faith believe will be saved and receive God free gift of grace. (Eph. 2:8-9)

Calvinism Distorts the Glory of God

A good example of the distorted extremes of the Calvinist is that they profoundly proclaim the marvelous glory of God while distorting this very truth. For example: this author watched Mark Kielar, a passionate Calvinist of the TV program "Word Pictures" aired on Cross TV, proclaimed that God shows His glory to those to whom He gives His grace, by sending those who are not allowed to believe and receive His grace to the Lake of Fire! What a completely warped idea he has of God's majesty and glory.

In other words, Kielar said that God, in saving some by irresistible grace and sending everyone else to an eternal hell, does so because He is sovereign and in doing so shows His glory?! That sounds like the actions of a tyrant and not a loving and just God. Thus, Kielar concludes that God shows how much He loves His "elect" by sending those He does not love to hell and by tormenting them for infinity. That shows the extent to which the Calvinist will goes to "justify" his perverted and distorted view of God.

Let me explain further: Yes, man is responsible and stands in condemnation for his sins. Those who reject God's grace do so because they love their sins more than their souls. (John 3:19-20) But to say that God is sovereign and because HE is sovereign He can act anyway He desires is a prevision of God's very character. If in His sovereignty He has chosen to withhold His offer of grace, and thereby will not allow the condemned to be saved, then makes God must share in the blame for those who reject Him. There is no glory in that for God.

Calvinism is a distorted, false theology that denies the very nature of God and, His plan of salvation and degrades God and His glory by making Him unloving and unjust. This vein of thinking is at least cult like because it distorts the loving and just character of God. In the place of our true Creator, they worship a God that says He loves, but at the same time acts unloving. God absolutely condemns sin and will destroy those who rebel against Him and refuse His grace. But the Bible never says men do not have the chance to repent and be saved because God would not allow them to.

To bring a man into the world and give him life who is already condemned to hell is absolutely an unloving act. No matter how hard the Calvinist tries to explain this away, this is the heart of his theology. It is a fact that to send a man to the Lake of Fire and not allow Him any chance for redemption is without question unloving. God says He died for the sins of all the world as 1 John 2:2 states. Jesus said that if a man would believe in Him, his sins would be forgiven and he would have everlasting life and not perish. (John 3:15-16, 36, Acts 2:21) The word believe means to "to have faith, to entrust, commit or put ones trust in." (Strong's 4102) These actions of a man's will that are based on his trust in the One in whom he is believing and entrusting himself to. It is God who seeks the lost and initiates His offer of salvation. Jesus said:

> *"No man can come to me, except the Father which hath sent me draw him: and I will raise him up at the last day". (John 6:44)*

Romans 1:18-23 explains that God reveals Himself to every man, and therefore a man who ends up condemned in hell is there because he rejected God's offer. The passages states this is the reason the wrath of God rests on the one who reject His grace. Jesus said,

> *"And this is the condemnation, that light is come into the world, and men loved darkness rather than light, because their deeds were evil. For every one that doeth evil hateth the light, neither cometh to the light, lest his deeds should be reproved." (John 3:19-20)*

The Cause of a Man's Condemnation

The cause of a man's condemnation is because he willingly rejects God's free offer of mercy and grace. To labor the point, it boils down to this. If God gave life to a man, but prior to that decreed that He would not allow the man to be saved and withholds His offer of grace, then the blame for the condemnation rests with God, and not wholly with the man. If God created a man to burn in the fires of hell and will not allow him to be saved, then the condemned man is doing the only thing God will allow him to do, and God is responsible for the man's condemnation. Clearly, this defies logic and cannot be the case. According to Calvinism, a man sins because God will not allow him to do otherwise. This is totally foreign to our glorious Creator, Savior, and God.

Most Calvinists in the pew do not take the time to consider what their false teachers are telling them, especially those of renown. Some of the ardent proponents of Calvinism, by their actions show that they have a distorted and false view of God and His plan of salvation. Calvinism may outwardly present the Gospel, but they clearly do not understand it or even biblically believe it. This deceives many people as these popular teachers eloquently teach the grace of God, but they do not explain their distorted and unbiblical view of it.

David Jeremiah

Recently, I was surprised to hear David Jeremiah fervently preach a message on the love of God from his current series promoting his book *"God Loves You."* I read the following in the Introduction to the book he was offering to his audience,

> "I did some checking on what kinds of books were being published, particularly books about God. And I was surprised that the simple message of God's love was being largely ignored. I knew what God wanted me to do. He wanted me to tell people, in the midst of such dark times, that God loves them; that He always has loved them; and that He always will love them. The title came together in my mind— something that doesn't always happen up front in the writing process: God Loves You: He Always Has— He Always Will."[46]

However, nowhere in his book does he mention election, predestination, or TULIP. He failed to mention that he believes God's love is only extended to the few who He decreed or were elected to receive His grace, but not to all the world. He proclaimed that if a man would believe, then Jesus Christ, God would forgive his sins and give him eternal life. Yet, this famous preacher was in reality was offering salvation to many in the audience that he believes cannot be saved because they were not elected to salvation. The Calvinist has no rival in preaching piety or God's sovereignty. Yet while the Calvinists are proclaiming God's glory, they are degrading Him and making Him like the other unloving and false god's of men's imaginations.

Does Calvinism Give a Biblical Explanation of Election?

The beliefs of the Calvinistic system of theology misinterpret the Bible's teaching on election. However, biblically election does refer to salvation as they contend, but to what salvation accomplishes in the life of the one who believes. Election is God's plan for what He desired would be the benefit of those who believed and put their faith in Him. Election then is God's plan or blueprint of salvation. Election is not what individual God will save, but what salvation would mean to those who accept His grace.

This is explained in Ephesians One. Verse 3 introduces the subject and content of the discourse.

> *"Blessed be the God and Father of our Lord Jesus Christ, who hath blessed us with all spiritual blessings in heavenly places in Christ" (Ephesians 1:3)*

Paul is addressing how wonderful (blessed) is

78

God who has blessed us with spiritual blessing in heavenly places in Christ. This is addressed to believers to remind them of the blessing of salvation to those "in Christ." Verses 4-6 explain the blessing that God gives to believers and what salvation is to achieve in their lives.

> "According as he hath chosen us in him before the foundation of the world, that we should be holy and without blame before him in love: Having predestinated us unto the adoption of children by Jesus Christ to himself, according to the good pleasure of his will, To the praise of the glory of his grace, wherein he hath made us accepted in the beloved." (Ephesians 1:4-6)

God has chosen "us," meaning those who are saved, before He created the world, that the believer should be holy (separated) and without blame (forgiven all sins) before Him in love. God's plan was that before the world existed, to make salvation a blessing to those who believed and received His grace by making those who are saved a part of the family of God, His children. The verse does not say or even imply that God chose which individual He would save, but to what salvation would impart to them. God is stating His blueprint for salvation. He is not saying that He is choosing some and rejecting others. There is not one hint of such a thought.

Verse 5 says God predestinated that believers would be "unto" (eis) the children adopted by Jesus Christ by the "good pleasure of His purpose will."(eudokia) In other words, God purposed that believers would be the adopted children of God. The statement does not address who God would save, but the relationship of the believer who is saved. Verse 6 states "To the praise of the glory of his grace, wherein he hath made us accepted in the beloved." (Ephesians 1:6) God's plan that He chose, was that those who are saved would be holy, without blame, and they would be the adopted children of God. Therefore it is His plan that is in view, not who would He would save. His plan, which is the blessing that is being proclaimed, is that those who by faith received God's gift of grace are "to the praise of the glory of his grace." It is God's grace, meaning His mercy and love, that are to His praise and glory. God is glorified in His benevolence (grace) and love toward sinful men. Verse 7 continues, proclaiming the basis of redemption, that God's plan is that the believer is made acceptable unto God through Jesus Christ's blood, being forgiven of his sins though the distribution (kata) of the "riches of His grace." That certainly does not sound like God is limiting His grace, but rather abundantly offering it to those who will accept it.

Neither this passage nor the New Testament says God elected or chose who would be saved or to whom He would deny His grace. The glory of His grace is that it is freely offered to all. This can be seen in the many passages of God's word stating that Christ died for all men. Calvinism teaches that election or God's gift of grace is limited to a select few whom God chooses to save. The Bible teaches that Jesus Christ died for the sins of the whole world and offers salvation to all who will believe. Note that this truth is plainly taught in the following verses:

"And he is the propitiation for our sins: and not for ours only, but also for the sins of the whole world" (1 John 2:2).

"For God so loved the world, that he gave his only begotten Son, that whosoever believeth in him should not perish, but have everlasting life" (John 3:16).

"For this is good and acceptable in the sight of God our Savior; Who will have all men to be saved, and to come unto the knowledge of the truth" (1 Timothy 2:4).

"Who (speaking of Christ) *gave himself a ransom for all, to be testified in due time"* (1 Timothy 2:6).

"For the love of Christ constraineth us; because we thus judge, that if one died for all, then were all dead" (2 Corinthians 5:14).

"And he said unto them, Go ye into all the world, and preach the gospel to every creature" (Mark 16:15).

"The Lord is not slack concerning his promise, as some men count slackness; but is longsuffering to us-ward, not willing that any should perish but that all should come to repentance" (2 Peter 3:9).

"And the times of this ignorance God winked at; but now commandeth all men every where to repent" (Acts 17:30).

"Therefore as by the offense of one judgment came upon all men to condemnation; even so by the righteousness of one the free gift came upon all men unto justification of life" (Romans 5:18).

> *"But we see Jesus, who was made a little lower than the angels for the suffering of death, crowned with glory and honor; that he by the grace of God should taste death for every man" (Hebrews 2:9).*

Clearly, each of these Scriptures teaches that Christ died for the sins of all men everywhere and wishes all men to be saved. Any teaching of man that contradicts this truth is false, and that should settle the matter.

It is understood that those that hold to limited atonement often counter by saying "the world" and "all men" does not mean the entire world or all men, but refers only to the "elect." Surely, such a line of thinking is based on man's faulty reasoning and not on sound hermeneutical principles. The clear meaning of the word "world" (cosmos), as used in the Bible, means the whole earth and everyone on it or the lost world. It is never used in the Bible as referring to God's elect or those who are saved. The word "all" is all-inclusive. "All men" encompasses everyone. If God had wanted to limit the scope of salvation, He could have easily chosen a better word than "all", "world" and "every" man! He chose these words because they convey the meaning that God intended. He paid the price for all men's sin everywhere in the entire world! He bought with His own blood the right to offer all men salvation. Limited atonement would imply he only suffered for those that will be saved, and this clearly an unbiblical teaching.

The Calvinist must disagree with many portions of God's Word to continue to teach that Christ's death was limited to only a few men who would be saved.

Matthew 7:13-14 and Romans 3:10-26 explains why men are lost and are condemned to hell. Romans 1:18-22 says:

"For the wrath of God is revealed from heaven against all ungodliness and unrighteousness of men, who hold the truth in unrighteousness; Because that which may be known of God is manifest in them; for God hath shewed it unto them. For the invisible things of him from the creation of the world are clearly seen, being understood by the things that are made, even his eternal power and Godhead; so that they are without excuse: Because that, when they knew God, they glorified him not as God, neither were thankful; but became vain in their imaginations, and their foolish heart was darkened" (Rom. 1:18-22)

The verse says that God's wrath is revealed from heaven against men's sin and that man holds the truth in unrighteousness. It states that God has revealed Himself to all men and therefore all men are without excuse. This begs the question . . . "Why would God reveal Himself to all men and base His wrath on the fact that men know the truth, but reject it, IF some men could not respond to God's revelation of Himself?"

Furthermore, the Calvinist must conclude that when he preaches the Gospel and presents salvation to his listeners, he is doing so "tongue in cheek." He must admit he is offering something that some hearing him cannot receive because God will not permit them to. I listened to a popular radio preacher eloquently speaking on the love of God for sinners for about fifteen minutes and then tell his audience that if they would believe in Jesus Christ they would be saved. Yet, as a Calvinist, his teaching contradicts his proclaiming of receiving salvation based on whether a person would believe. This radio and television preacher, because of his belief in Calvinism, does not believe that most who hear his messages can be saved because he believes God has chosen to withhold grace to most of the world and thus condemned them without any hope of salvation. The Gospel then becomes "Good News", only to the select few. The others, whom the Calvinist says are born for hell, are wasting their time even hearing of Christ's death, burial and resurrection, because they cannot receive Christ. They are, according to Calvinism, elected by God to an unalterable course to hell. I heard John MacArthur on the radio clearly and passionately present the Gospel. He calls his programs "Grace to You," but plainly believes that God's grace is only for the "few." What is baffling me is the fact that he and the Calvinists cannot see the contradiction in their beliefs and message.

Some Errors of John Piper

For example, in his message on "God so loved the World- Part 1, John 3:16" John Piper states, "For God so loved the world . . ." The most common meaning for world in John is the created and fallen totality of mankind. John 7:7: "The world cannot hate you, but it hates me because I testify about it that its works are evil." John 14:17 states:

> *". . . the Spirit of truth, whom the world cannot receive, because it neither sees him nor knows him."*

That is the way John is using world here. The word refers to the great mass of fallen humanity that needs salvation. It is the countless number of perishing people from whom the "whosoever" come in the second part of the verse: ". . . that whoever believes in him should not perish." The world is the great ocean of perishing sinners from whom the whoever comes."[47]

Yet, in another message, Piper says about God's love:

> "It's not a saving love that he has for everybody. Else everybody would be saved, since they would not have to meet any conditions, not even faith."[48]

Can there be any question that what Piper believes and what he preaches is a contradiction?

To labor the point, if Calvinism is true, the Calvinists who preaches, teaches, and witnesses to the Gospel is in reality, according to Calvinism, lying to most of the people who hear him and he's doing so in Jesus' name. It is a lie to tell a man that if he will believe in Jesus Christ that he shall be saved (Romans 10:9-10) while, at the same time, believing and teaching that most cannot accept Christ because God will not allow them to be saved. According to Calvinism, the unelected are not offered God's grace, and most of the human race is doomed to hell with no chance of redemption. Technically and practically it is a lie to tell an unelected person he can be saved when he cannot.

In all the literature I have read I have never found

where the Calvinists gives any criteria for determining who is elected and who is not. The reason is clear . . . not even the Calvinist would go that far in their false teaching. Doctrinal error perverts God's truth and corrupts the very Gospel the Calvinist claims he believes. The questions the Calvinist must answer are these: "How do you know someone is elected? On what basis do you make such a determination?" Jesus speaking to Israel warned them that the inhabitants of Sodom and Gomorrah would receive less punishment in the day of judgment, because Israel had the privilege of seeing and hearing the Messiah, but rejected Him.(See Matthew 10:15) He said the same thing of Chorazin and Bethsaida warning them of the results of their rejection of their Christ.

> *"Woe unto thee, Chorazin! woe unto thee, Bethsaida! for if the mighty works had been done in Tyre and Sidon, which have been done in you, they had a great while ago repented, sitting in sackcloth and ashes" (Luke 10:13).*

Jesus stated that their condemnation was because they had seen His miracles and heard His message, but had rejected Him as their Messiah. This clear truth is but another death blow to the heresy of Calvinism. Clearly, the people in these two cities, where Jesus presented the Gospel, willingly rejected the truth that they heard from Jesus Himself. Because of their rejection, Jesus said they would be judged more harshly than those who had not been privileged to hear the truth. If the people in these cities in Israel could not have responded to the truth after hearing it, because they were predestined by

God to Hell, then on what basis could God judge them more harshly than those who had not heard? Doubtlessly, God held them accountable for their sin of rejecting the truth and in doing so verified that they could have responded, but chose not to. It was not God who chose to send them to hell simply because He could do so and because He decreed their condemnation. The people of these two cities condemned themselves because of their willing unbelief.

CHAPTER EIGHT

PASSAGES THAT THE CALVINISTS USE TO SUPPORT THEIR THEOLOGY

Matthew 28:19-20 The Great Commission

The Great Commission stated in Matthew 28:19-20 "to go into all the world and teach the Gospel" loses its purpose in Calvinistic teaching. Jesus' last words recorded in Acts 1:8 proclaim:

> *"But ye shall receive power, after that the Holy Ghost is come upon you: and ye shall be witnesses unto me both in Jerusalem, and in all Judaea, and in Samaria, and unto the uttermost part of the earth." (Acts 1:8)*

Why teach salvation to all the world if God is going to save the elect anyway? The Calvinist again will counter by saying that God commands us to preach the Gospel and that is God's method to reach the elect. Again this is an example of the poor reasoning behind Calvinism and, indeed, a failure in human reasoning. If the Bible teaches that we are to tell all men everywhere they can be saved by trusting in Christ Jesus and God, but in fact has limited the offer to only a select few, then we become liars and God is sending us out into the "uttermost part of the earth" with a tainted message! Please excuse the redundancy in the following statement, but it is a lie for a man to stand before an audience and preach that God will save those that hear him if they will believe and put their trust in Jesus Christ, if God has elected that some of them cannot respond! God is not the author of lies; Satan is the author of the sin of lying (John 8:44). What a gross insult to the truth and to Almighty God to make God a liar and His evangelists a party to it, though this false teaching.

Does John 11:49-52 Teach Limited Atonement?

According to John 11:49-52, it seems that a good number of Jews, upon seeing Jesus' miracle, believed in Him. One of the miracles the Jews had just witnessed was raising Lazarus from the grave. Some who saw the miracle went to their religious leaders, seeking advice and to understand what was happening. They were confused because the Jewish rulers were seeking to kill Jesus and denounced Him, even saying He performed His miracles by demons. Thus, the people saw the miracles He performed and knew only One from God could do these supernatural acts, and they were confused.

The chief priests and the Pharisees of the Sanhedrin met under pressure from and worried about what would be the consequences of Jesus' miracles and message would be to them to decide what to do. They were afraid of the problem Jesus was causing. It is important to understand the context. The rulers of the Jews served at the discretion of their Roman conquerors. Israel was looking for a civil Messiah and not a spiritual One as Jesus was. John 6:15 states this saying,

"When Jesus therefore perceived that they

would come and take him by force, to
make him a king, he departed again into a
mountain himself alone." (John 6:15)

The Jews, and even His disciples, did not see Him as God come to suffer and die for the sins of the world, but as a national hero with great power to throw off the Roman oppression and free Israel from its enemies. (Read John 7:1-5)

Therefore seeing Jesus as a civil Messiah and not really believing He could overcome the Roman rule of Israel, they concluded that Jesus should be destroyed before He could bring down the wrath of Rome on them. Furthermore, they were afraid also that they would lose their position of power in Israel if Jesus did overthrow the Romans. They were merely using their supposed concern for Israel to hide their true intent, which was to destroy the Lord who was exposing their gross sin and hypocrisy. (see Matt. 23:13-29) Thus, in verse 51, John states Caiaphas foretold that they (they Jewish rulers) would sacrifice Jesus to appease the Romans and thus spare the Jews from Roman reprisals.

Verse 52 is John's addition to Caiaphas' statement. Caiaphas did not make the statement of verse 52. John stated this would be the result of the high priest's prediction. In other words, Caiaphas' and the Sanhedrin's decision was to put Jesus to death and that His death would be for the Jews in Jerusalem, and around the world. In verse 53, the Jewish rulers from that day made the decision to put Jesus to death and in their minds, they were doing so to save Israel from the Romans.

There is absolutely nothing in this passage that teaches or even hints at Limited Atonement. Yet, this is the tactic of false teachers. I have often wondered, why does the Calvinist go to such extraordinary lengths to "prove" his false theology. Wouldn't it make more sense just to believe God's word and literally accept His truth?

Does John 12:40 support Calvinism?

> *"That the saying of Esaias the prophet might be fulfilled, which he spake, Lord, who hath believed our report? and to whom hath the arm of the Lord been revealed? Therefore they could not believe, because that Esaias said again, He hath blinded their eyes, and hardened their heart; that they should not see with their eyes, nor understand with their heart, and be converted, and I should heal them. These things said Esaias, when he saw his glory, and spake of him." (John 12:38-41)*

The statement:

> *"Therefore they could not believe, because that Esaias said again, He hath blinded their eyes, and hardened their heart; that they should not see with their eyes, nor understand with their heart, and be converted, and I should heal them"*

must be interpreted in the analogy of the faith. John quotes Isaiah 6:9-10 which is quoted six times in the New Testament. (Matt. 13:14-15; Mark 4:12; Luke 8:10; Acts 28:26-27; Rom. 11:8) At first reading it seems that the passage is saying God is the cause of their unbelief because He blinded their eyes so they could not see and be saved and healed. However this interpretation is inconsistent with other statements of God's desire to see all men believe and be saved. God cannot contradict Himself so this is not the correct interpretation. God states that His desire is that none perish and all come to repentance.

> "The Lord is not slack concerning his promise, as some men count slackness; but is longsuffering to us-ward, not willing that any should perish, but that all should come to repentance." (2 Peter 3:9)

It would be a contradiction of God's word for Him to desire that no one perish, and then to blind their eyes to the truth, thus preventing them from believing and being saved. Therefore, we must look closer for God's meaning.

Why Men Are Condemned

Jesus explained why men are condemned, saying,

> "And this is the condemnation, that light is come into the world, and men loved darkness rather than light, because their deeds were evil. For every one that doeth evil hateth the light, neither cometh to the light, lest his deeds should be reproved." (John 3:19-20)

Why did that Jesus say men reject the light? He says it is because their deeds are evil and they reject the truth because it exposes and reproves them of their sin. Note that Jesus plainly states that this is the reason that men are condemned. He does not say, nor does the Bible anywhere say, that God condemns men inadvertently by decreeing their condemnation to the Lake of Fire by withholding His grace. Nowhere does God say He predetermined and elected anyone to spend eternity in hell by withholding His grace and mercy. God is love and that false teaching of limited atonement contradicts the very nature of God who desires all men to be saved.

Luke Explains Man's Blindness

In Acts 28:27, Luke explains why men's eyes are blinded.

> "For the heart of this people is waxed gross, and their ears are dull of hearing, and _their eyes have they closed_; lest they should see with their eyes, and hear with their ears, and understand with their heart, and should be converted, and I should heal them."

Note the underlined words "their eyes have they closed." It was their willing unbelief that prevented them from seeing the truth and accepting it. Those who refused to believe were not converted because they did not want God in their lives or to be saved.

God did blind their eyes and hardened their hearts, but it was because they refused to believe. In other words, they refused to believe in God and therefore, He honored their desire and stopped seeking to bring them to salvation. What He blinded their eyes to was to spiritual truth. The unsaved do not understand God's word or spiritual things. Paul explains this saying,

> "But the natural man receiveth not the things of the Spirit of God: for they are

94

> *foolishness unto him: neither can he know them, because they are spiritually discerned." (1 Corinthians 2:14)*

God will not let the lost man see more than the truth of the Gospel. Only the saved born again believer who has the new nature and the indwelling of the Holy Spirit can see the deep things of God.

> *"But God hath revealed them unto us by his Spirit: for the Spirit searcheth all things, yea, the deep things of God." (1 Corinthians 2:10)*

Does John 15:16 teach that God only chose some for salvation?

Always in interpreting God's word, one must consider the context of the statement, that is, who is being addressed and what is the situation. Jesus was speaking to His disciples whom He had chosen. (John 6:70, 13:18, 15:19). He was not making a general statement as to their salvation. They were saved, except for Judas as John 6:70 states. Jesus was expressing His choosing them for service so that they would "go and bring forth fruit, and that your fruit should remain." Furthermore, He promised to fulfill their requests in prayer for help in fulfilling His commission to them. The choosing was to service...not to salvation as the words state.

Serious Mistakes of Interpretation

One of the most serious mistakes made by those that misinterpret God's word is to ignore biblical hermeneutical principles of interpretation. The context, grammar, analogy of the faith, historical and cultural details are vital to making a proper interpretation. Ignoring these principles is the foundation of false doctrines such as Calvinism.[49]

What do Verses Acts 17:30-31 teach?

Acts 17:30-31, explains:

"And the times of this ignorance God winked at; but now commandeth all men every where to repent: Because he hath appointed a day, in which he will judge the world in righteousness by that man whom he hath ordained; whereof he hath given assurance unto all men, in that he hath raised him from the dead."

In this verse, God commands "all" men "everywhere" to repent. As shown earlier, the use of the words "all" and "everywhere" makes it undoubtedly clear that this command is not limited to a select few, but to everyone, everywhere and none are excluded. This passage teaches that man is responsible and will be judged for his sins. The basis of this judgment is the fact that Christ came into the world and brought salvation. Taking away man's responsibility to receive Christ as Savior takes away a man's chance to be saved. Taking away God's offer of grace leaves God without a basis for judgment. God cannot unjustly condemn a man for not receiving something he was unable to receive. Revelation 20:12 states, that at the final judgment of the lost, the unsaved will be judged according to their works, and not because God decreed their damnation. How could a just God judge men according to their works when, because of His sovereign choice, He decreed them only able to do sinful works, since He had denied salvation to them?

God says,

> *"He that believeth on him is not condemned: but he that believeth not is condemned already, because he hath not believed in the name of the only begotten Son of God." (John 3:18)*

The false conclusion of Calvinism is that some cannot be saved, because God decreed their damnation. This verse says the unsaved are condemned because they would not believe. Calvinism denies this biblical truth. The teaching of the Bible regarding the nature of God shows us that He cannot be just if He decrees some to hell without the possibility of their accepting or rejecting God.

Going back to the many verses stating that Christ died for the sins of the "world," one must assume that Christ's death was for the of salvation of those who believe and at the same time the grounds of condemnation for those who do not believe.[50] The basis of man's condemnation is that man is a sinner and justly deserves hell. That is mirrored by the marvelous love of God that offers man redemption, but it does not force him to receive it. If a man, under the convicting and enabling ministry of the Holy Spirit responds, his sins are forgiven completely; he becomes a child of God and receives eternal life.

> *"And the times of this ignorance God winked at; but now commandeth all men every where [emphasis added] to repent: Because he hath appointed a day, in the which he will judge the world in righteousness by that man whom he hath ordained; whereof he hath given assurance unto all men , in that he hath raised him from the dead" (Acts 17:31).*

Does Romans 8:29-30 support Calvinism?

"For whom he did foreknow, he also did predestinate to be conformed to the image of his Son, that he might be the first born among many brethren. Moreover whom he did predestinate, them he also called: and whom he called, them he also justified: and whom he justified, them he also glorified." (Rom. 8:29-30).

There is much debate over what God's foreknowledge means. The word "foreknow" is the Greek word "proginsko" ("pro" = before and "gingko" means "to know"). The definition of the word is simple, meaning "to know beforehand." God is omniscient and knows all things past, present and future. God is not subject to time and sees all things as present. The problem is that the Calvinist defines foreknowledge as being determinative. In other words, the Calvinists conclude that if God fore knows something, it means He causes it to happen.

In Romans 8:29, the Lord used two words to convey His truth. He said,

"For whom he did foreknow, he also did predestinate."

The wording of the verse communicates two separate actions. One, God knew through His omniscience who would believe in the Lord Jesus Christ. Second, those He foreknew would believe, He predestinated "to be conformed to the image of Jesus Christ." If foreknowledge was causative He would not have stated that He predestinated what they would become. Because God knows the future ahead of time, it does not mean He makes it happen. In His foreknowledge he also knows what would happen under different circumstances. For example, in 1 Samuel 23:12, David asked the Lord if the men of Keilah would hand him over to Saul. God replied that they would hand him over to Saul. However, it never happened. David and his men left and went into the mountains of Ziph. God's foreknowledge is simply that He is omniscient and knows all things without the limitation of time. But God's foreknowledge does not make an event happen. Proper hermeneutical principles would dictate that a passage be interpreted literally, observing the definition of the words and their grammatical construction within the sentences. In other words, we must take the statement literally at its face value. Commenting on the word "foreknowledge" Barnes says:

> "The literal meaning of the word cannot be a matter of dispute. It denotes, properly, to know beforehand; to be acquainted with future events."[51]

The question is, "What does the word "election" refer to and what did God predestinate?" God is omniscient, and the verse says God foreknew those who would be saved and He predestinated them "to be conformed to the image of his Son." The verse does not say God predestined those He foreknew to be saved. Rather, He states that those who are saved are to be conformed to the image of His Son.

The word "conformed" means "to be made unto like fashion." God's plan is that believers are to be made in like fashion to Christ, meaning to be like Christ and to live godly lives.

1 John 3:2 states that believers will be like Christ,

"we shall be like him; for we shall see him as he is."

Election then explains God's plan for those who believe and whom He saves. God's election did not pertain to which individuals would be saved, but what to salvation would bring to those who are saved.

Paul, in Romans 8, states several blessings that God's predestined plan gives the believer. Please note that these truths are in the context of Romans 8:28-29. The believer becomes a spiritual being as Christ,

> "But ye are not in the flesh, but in the Spirit, if so be that the Spirit of God dwell in you. Now if any man have not the Spirit of Christ, he is none of his." (Romans 8:9)

Additionally, Paul explains that the ones who believe are made joint heirs with Jesus Christ.

> "And if children, then heirs; heirs of God, and joint-heirs with Christ; if so be that we suffer with him, that we may be also glorified together." (Romans 8:17)

Romans 8:29 explains that this is God's plan as to what believers become in Christ. Ephesians 2:10, states:

> "For we are his workmanship, created in Christ Jesus unto good works, which God hath before ordained that we should walk in them."

The Result of Salvation Establishes Election

Election or "fore-ordination" established the result of salvation for those who will believe in Jesus Christ. It ordained that those who believe would be made alive (given eternal life) and declared in God's favor forever. The Calvinist, in his blindsided view of Scripture, concludes that this verse means election is to salvation by God. Election rightly refers to the plan of what salvation accomplishes for the believer, not to whom God offers His grace, or from whom He withholds it.

The context of Romans 8:28 addresses God's plan in salvation, that, "And we know that all things work together for good to them that love God, to them who are the called according to his purpose." (Romans 8:28) God is revealing the result of His plan of salvation, in that He is working in every believer's life. This is expounded further in verses 31-39, which teach assurance of salvation based on the work and plan of God.

The context of verse 29-30 is clear. God is talking about a Christian living within the purposes of God. He is referring to His plan for believers. He is certainly not telling us that He chooses only to save certain individuals and chooses to condemn the rest to Hell. The passage does not say or even infer that idea. In other words, God is saying He is in control of all that salvation is deemed to accomplish in the life of a believer. It is God's plan that whatever happens to the believer will work out for good. Furthermore, the verse says this is applicable to those who are "called according to his purposes". What purposes? The answer is the part of His purpose that all things work for good in a believer's life. The verse does not address who will be allowed to receive salvation, but the circumstances of life that the believer faces and their result. God is saying that believers are called by

Him to live according to His plan. It is the plan of what God purposed salvation to accomplish that is in view; not who would be saved.

Verses 29-30 continue the discussion and state that God predestined, or to say it another way, God planned that believers were to be conformed to the image of Christ. That means to grow or strive to live like Christ. Christ is the standard that believers are to live by and judge their lives. Again, the verse is not talking about initial salvation but rather God's plan for the believer after salvation.

In verse 30, God says those whom He foreknew, He called, justified and glorified. Here is the work of God in salvation. Those who God foreknew would believe through in His omniscience, He called justified and glorified. God plainly states that the calling, justification and glorification was for those who He foreknew would believe and be saved. Then, in the next verse, God gives absolute assurance to the believer that God is working in his life, not only in salvation, but in eternal security. The believer is assured that God will carry out His plan.

In 1 John 5:13, the Lord bases assurance of salvation on one's belief in the name of the Son of God. The verse says,

> *"These things have I written unto you that believe on the name of the Son of God; that ye may know that ye have eternal life, and that ye may believe on the name of the Son of God."*

Assurance

The basis of assurance of salvation given in the New Testament is one's belief in Jesus Christ. It is never presented as being based on election to salvation by God. A person knows he is saved because he truly believes in Jesus Christ, not because he was elected to salvation by God. There is not one word, stated or implied in Romans 8:29-30 that says God predestined some to salvation and the rest He condemned to Hell.

Does Roman 9 Support Calvinism?

Often the Calvinists refer to Romans 9 as proof of their false view of election. However, to properly understand the statements of this chapter we must first consider the context and subject being addressed. The context of Romans 9 is Paul's answer to the question of Romans 3:1,

> "What advantage then has the Jew? or
> "what profit is there of circumcision?"

This discourse begins with this question and ends with Romans 11. Paul is addressing the misunderstanding of the Jews in which they concluded that they were in God's favor because they were born Hebrews, God's chosen people, and were assured of heaven and of God's grace.

An Example: Nicodemus

John 3:1-7 is an example of this error in Jewish thinking and was the reason for Jesus' response to Nicodemus. Jesus explained to this Pharisee that he must be "born again". Nicodemus believed that he was going to heaven and would be a part of God's kingdom because he was born a Jew. Jesus said, "Not so." A man must be born of water (human birth) and of the Spirit (spiritual birth) to be saved. He was saying to Nicodemus, in order to be saved you must be spiritually reborn and that happens when a person believes on the Lord Jesus Christ. In John 3:15-16, Jesus continues and explains how to be saved by faith. Paul explains in Romans 3-11, that the Jew, like the Gentile, is responsible to God and the Jew's only advantage is that he has been born among a people who God chose to reveal Himself through thus they had the knowledge of God. But being a Jew does not ensure salvation, because as Paul plainly states in Chapter 10:9-10 salvation is a matter of faith.

An Example: Esau

Many teach that Romans 9:13-14 states that God rejected and condemned Esau to hell, but chose to save Jacob.

> *"As it is written, Jacob have I loved, but Esau have I hated."*

However, this is not what the verse is saying. Paul is not talking about God predestining or in His sovereignty decreeing Jacob to heaven and Esau to hell. God chooses to "use" some in His plan, such as Jacob and others, such as Esau, to "reject."

The term "hated" used in Romans 9:13 means to "love less or to choose instead of."   It does not mean to condemn. Jesus in Luke 14:26 uses the same word stating,

> *"If any man come to me, and hate not his father, and mother, and wife, and children, and brethren, and sisters, yea, and his own life also, he cannot be my disciple."*

Clearly, God does not require that we "hate" our family, but in using the term He means that we are to choose Him first or to place Him before our relatives. God is also not saying He simply hated Esau and sent him to hell. God is saying he chose to reject Esau and He had good reasons. What God is revealing is related to His plan of bringing salvation through the Jews, mainly through Abraham, Isaac and Jacob. God is to have preeminence in our lives as Colossians 1:18, instructs and those are the people He uses in His plans.

The word "hate" means to "love less," and in Romans 9, God uses the illustration of His choosing Jacob rather than Esau to illustrate the point that being born a Jew does not save a person. God says that He rejected to use Esau, the first born son, because he was not a man who loved or served God. His interests in life were worldly and did not include the Lord. Further, the promise made to Abraham would normally be through his first born son. This promise was God's plan for the coming nation of Israel and the Messiah. However, Esau showed no interest in his birth right and the sacredness of God's promise. He thought so little of it; he sold it for a bowl of pottage. Therefore, God rejected him as the natural heir of Abraham and Isaac and as the one through whom God would bring the Messiah who would be the Savior. The verse does not teach that God just choose to hate Esau, or that God in His sovereignty decreed to send him to hell as Calvinism teaches! God did not decree to "hate" Esau, but rather He rejected Esau because he rejected God. A false interpretation of God's word always leads to confusion and false doctrine.

Consider this. Suppose there are two brothers in

a family. One is a rebel and always in trouble. The other is a Christian and lives for the Lord. Who would God chose then to serve Him? God being omniscient, would He choose the rebellious son who rejected God and His purpose for his life, or the faithful one who believed in God?

It should also be understood that the names Jacob and Esau also refer to the progeny of both men. The Book of Obadiah makes this perfectly clear that God rejected the "house of Esau," who were the enemies of the house of Jacob. God said He would destroy completely the house of Esau (also called Edom, Mt. Seir), and none of them would remain (Obadiah 17-18). The decedents of Esau hated God, and for generations they opposed Israel (Jacob) until God finally destroyed them. Hermeneutically, the passage is correctly interpreted in its context as referring to the Nation of Edom (Esau), not strictly to Esau who fathered the nation.

Correctly Interpreting Romans 9:20-21

Romans 9:20-21 is also a passage that is misunderstood and incorrectly used to support Calvinism's false idea that God predestined some to hell.

> "What shall we say then? Is there unrighteousness with God? God forbid. For he saith to Moses, I will have mercy on whom I will have mercy, and I will have compassion on whom I will have compassion. So then it is not of him that willeth, nor of him that runneth, but of God that sheweth mercy. For the scripture saith unto Pharaoh, Even for

> *this same purpose have I raised thee up,*
> *that I might shew my power in thee, and*
> *that my name might be declared*
> *throughout all the earth. Therefore hath*
> *he mercy on whom he will have mercy,*
> *and whom he will he hardeneth. Thou*
> *wilt say then unto me, Why doth he yet*
> *find fault? For who hath resisted his will?*
> *Nay but, O man, who art thou that*
> *repliest against God? Shall the thing*
> *formed say to him that formed it, Why*
> *hast thou made me thus? Hath not the*
> *potter power over the clay, of the same*
> *lump to make one vessel unto honour,*
> *and another unto dishonour?"*

Vessels For Destruction

God is the "author and finisher of our faith." (Hebrews 12:2) It is His plan and in His sovereignty He has chosen what salvation is to be. Romans 9:20-23 is Paul's second answer to the question asked in verse 19,

> *"Thou wilt say then unto me, Why doth*
> *he yet find fault? For who hath resisted*
> *his will?"*

Vessels fitted for destruction are those that reject God. You cannot blame God for that, or make Him the cause of men's rejecting Him. Paul is addressing the Jews that rejected Jesus as the Messiah. These people, by their rejection of Christ made themselves "vessels fitted for destruction." Jesus fulfilled all the Old Testament prophecies as to His coming and work. He performed supernatural miracles that only God could do. (See John 3:1-2) Yet, in spite of all the signs and wonders God showed them, they rejected Him as their Messiah. Therefore, by their actions they condemned themselves. Nothing in the passages says God decreed to make them "vessels fitted for destruction." Romans 6:23 says,

> *"For the wages of sin is death; but the gift*
> *of God is eternal life through Jesus Christ*
> *our Lord."*

Does not God plainly state in 1 Timothy 2:4 that all men could be saved? How then can the Calvinist totally miss the point of the subject of Romans 9-11 and suppose that it supports the idea that God, in His sovereignty, chose to send some to hell, excluding them from his plan of salvation?

Paul uses the example of Pharaoh to illustrate his point. Pharaoh rejected God over and over, and that was the ruler's choice (Romans 9:17) Pharaoh refused to believe God and submit to Him. Is God to be blamed for Pharaoh ultimately rejecting God, especially after God showed him who He was by demonstrating His power repeatedly in bringing the plagues? God's bringing the plagues was God demonstrating His power to Pharaoh to persuade Him to obey God and let Israel go. Pharaoh could have believed and obeyed God, but he chose rather to reject Him in the face of overwhelming evidence. Paul asked the question, "What shall we say then? Is there unrighteousness with God? God forbid." (Rom. 9:14) In other words, is God at fault for Pharaoh's condemnation? The answer is "of course not" . . . Pharaoh condemned himself by rejecting God. There is plainly no support in this passage for God electing some to hell denying them the opportunity to believe and be saved.

The statement that God "hardened Pharaoh's heart" means that God permitted Pharaoh to resist Him. God did not make Pharaoh reject Him; that is the point Paul is making. Genesis 6:3, states that the Holy Spirit will not always "strive" with man. God does seek to guide and direct man, but in time, if the man resists God, the Holy Spirit will stop seeking to win Him and leave that man to his own devices. Man's rejection of God does not allow God to work; God will not violate a man's will. He will allow men to remain, as men choose, to be blind and hardened in their heart rejecting God. God further states,

> "What shall we say then? Is there unrighteousness with God? God forbid." (Romans 9:14)

God is not unrighteous which means He does that which is right. By God's own principles He is a God of mercy.

> "For he saith to Moses, I will have mercy on whom I will have mercy, and I will have compassion on whom I will have compassion. So then it is not of him that willeth, nor of him that runneth, but of God that sheweth mercy." (Romans 9:15-16)

The Example: Pharaoh

The Lord is saying that no one has any special hold on God because of who he is or his position. God's nature is to offer grace and to show mercy without restriction. That is exactly what He did with Pharaoh. He repeatedly revealed Himself to Pharaoh through the plagues. God was doing what was right and offering Him salvation. Pharaoh rejected God and refused to believe. Thus Pharaoh condemned Himself. The blame rests on Pharaoh, not God. God was righteous in offering His mercy to Pharaoh. It is a gross misinterpretation to suggest God that revealed Himself to Pharaoh all the while knowing He would not allow Pharaoh to respond in faith.

> *"For the scripture saith unto Pharaoh, Even for this same purpose have I raised thee up, that I might shew my power in thee, and that my name might be declare throughout all the earth." (Romans 9:17)*

If Pharaoh could not have responded then God would be unrighteous.

God is not to blame for the damnation of a man who chooses to be blind and harden his heart against the urging of the Holy Spirit. God has gone to great lengths to bring men to Himself (Romans 1:20-21). God does not force man to believe or accept Him. He allows them to resist and exercise their own wills. Pharaoh's heart was hardened because he was a sinful, proud man who would not give up his sin. He valued the slave labor of the Hebrews more than his own soul. He chose to reject God's truth as John 3:19-20 says,

> *"And this is the condemnation, that light is come into the world, and men loved darkness rather than light, because their deeds were evil. For every one that doeth evil hateth the light, neither cometh to the light, lest his deeds should be reproved."*

James 1:13-14 says that God does not tempt men. God presented to Pharaoh the truth of who He was and what was His will. He did not tempt Pharaoh with the intent to prevent Pharaoh from accepting Him. To the contrary He revealed Himself to the Egyptian ruler that he might believe. Pharaoh refused to believe God for his own reasons and the blame rests solely with him. Pharaoh was condemned by his unbelief and by his own sinful nature (John 3:19-20, James 1:14-15). Nothing in this passage supports the idea that God in His sovereignty has decreed who He would or would not allow to be saved. God did decree that all who believed would be saved.

Does Ephesians 1 Support the Calvinistic View of Election?

Ephesians 1 is another passage the Calvinist misuses to teach God chooses to save some and condemn others.

The Significance of "In Christ"

Let us examine the passage biblically. Ephesians 1:3-12:

> 3 "Blessed be the God and Father of our Lord Jesus Christ, who hath blessed us with all spiritual blessings in heavenly places in Christ: 4 According as he hath chosen us in him before the foundation of the world, that we should be holy and without blame before him in love: 5 Having predestined us unto the adoption of children by Jesus Christ to himself, according to the good pleasure of his will, 6 To the praise of the glory of his grace, wherein he hath made us accepted in the beloved. 7 In whom we have redemption through his blood, the forgiveness of

sins, according to the riches of his grace; 8 Wherein he hath abounded toward us in all wisdom and prudence; 9 Having made known unto us the mystery of his will, according to his good pleasure which he hath purposed in himself: 10 That in the dispensation of the fullness of times he might gather together in one all things in Christ, both which are in heaven, and which are on earth; even in him: 11 In whom also we have obtained an inheritance, being predestinated according to the purpose of him who worketh all things after the counsel of his own will: 12 That we should be to the praise of his glory, who first trusted in Christ. 13 In whom ye also trusted, after that ye heard the word of truth, the gospel of your salvation: in whom also after that ye believed, ye were sealed with that holy Spirit of promise, 14 Which is the earnest of our inheritance until the redemption of the purchased possession, unto the praise of his glory."

This passage in Ephesians deals with God's plan for the believer who is saved by faith. Verse 3 introduces the discourse and states that God has blessed believers with "spiritual blessings in heavenly places." Note that the word "blessings" is plural; therefore, it is referring not to a single blessing, but to multiple blessings. Verse 4 continues stating the believer is chosen **in Christ** before the foundations of the world to be holy and without blame before Him in love. The verse does not say a person is chosen "to" Christ but "in" Christ. The significance of using "in" instead of "to" means that the person who is saved and "in" Christ is chosen to accomplish a purpose of God. God is revealing what redemption would accomplish in the believer's life. His plan is that, through His love, God chose that believers would stand before Him. Specifically, the passage says,

> ". . . that we should be holy and without blame before him in love: Having predestinated us unto the adoption of children by Jesus Christ to himself, according to the good pleasure of his will, To the praise of the glory of his grace, wherein he hath made us accepted in the beloved." (Ephesians 1:4b-6)

What is accomplished by God's elected plan is that a believer would be holy, and without blame (forgiven of all sin).

Further, God predestinated through His plan that the believer would become an adopted child in the Lord Jesus Christ, which was God's good pleasure to grant. God is explaining that those who are saved become His children and part of His heavenly family. (See Col. 1:12, 3:24; Heb. 9:15; 1 Pet. 3-4) The believer then is elected to be to the praise and glory of His grace. All this God elected so that the believer becomes accepted in the "beloved" meaning Jesus Christ. This passage does not say that God chose these to be saved, but rather He chose what they would become when they were saved.

God's Plan for Believers

As in Romans 8:29-30, this passage explains that God's plan for believers in salvation is what is being addressed. These passages are not saying that God made a sovereign choice to call some to salvation and withhold that call from others. This passage does not state that God elected some to be born destined for hell, but rather presents God's plan for the believer's life in Christ.

Verse 9, reveals that this was a mystery, which is a truth not previously revealed, that in the fullness of time, His plan was that He would gather together in one, all things in Christ (v10). In the Old Testament, God instituted the nation of Israel to be His witness to the world and to be the people to whom the Messiah would be born. In Ephesians 1, God is revealing His previously undisclosed plan for the institution of the local church, which is the Bride and Body of Jesus Christ on earth. The special relationship with God, being in His family, was not offered to Israel. The word "family" is found seventy three times in the Old Testament, but it is never used to refer to Israel as God's family. Israel was never called the "the children of God." The believers in this dispensation of the Church Age are called the children of God six times. Believers today are in a special dispensation of being in the Body and Bride of Jesus Christ. (See Eph. 5:30, Rev. 21:9, 22:17) This is the truth God that reveals in this passage. He is certainly not stating that He only offers salvation to a select few who He elects to receive grace.

Verse 11 further explains that God's plan is that He willed or predestined "That we should be of his

114

glory, who first trusted in Christ" (v12). Believers are to bring glory to God, and this was a purpose of His plan or what God elected for those that would believe.

When Is A Believer Sealed?

Verses 12-13, which are addressed to believers, say,

"In whom ye also trusted, after that ye heard the word of truth, the gospel of your salvation: in whom also after that ye believed, ye were sealed with that holy Spirit of promise" (Ephesians 1:13)."

It is noteworthy that those who are saved are not sealed with the "Holy Spirit of promise" until they believe. This is an important point. Surely, if God had chosen them to be saved before the world existed, then in His sovereignty, He would have sealed them to salvation before they believed. Ephesians 1 is not saying God predestined some individuals to be saved and others lost. The passage states that God predestinated that all who believe would be saved and subsequently "sealed" with the "spirit of promise," meaning that they would not be lost. "He that believeth on the Son hath everlasting life: and he that believeth not the Son shall not see life; but the wrath of God abideth on him" (John 3:36).

Does 1 Peter 2:8-10 Support Calvinism?

"And a stone of stumbling, and a rock of offense, even to them which stumble at the word, being disobedient: whereunto also they were appointed. But ye are a chosen generation, a royal priesthood, an holy nation, a peculiar people; that ye

should shew forth the praises of him who hath called you out of darkness into his marvellous light: Which in time past were not a people, but are now the people of God: which had not obtained mercy, but now have obtained mercy." (1 Peter 2:8-10)

One major error of Calvinism is that it interprets the scriptures with the presupposition that Calvinism is a correct view. This eisegetical hermeneutic imposes an interpretation of the passage that fits this preconceived premise. The interpretation of a passage must be based on the definition of its words, grammatical construction, analogy of the faith, and its context. If these principles of interpretation are ignored it will produce an incorrect meaning. Applying proper principles of interpretation, note that the verse states that Christ to the unbeliever is,

". . . a stone of stumbling, and a rock of offense, even to them which stumble at the word, being disobedient." (2 Peter 2:8)

In other words, these people to whom this verse is referring heard the word and stumbled at it. The word "stumble" is the Greek word "proskopto" and means to "strike or surge against." They heard God's truth, yet they were deliberately disobedient to it. They knew it was God's word, but they refused to accept Him or His word. God then says ". . . whereunto they were appointed." The word "whereunto" refers to God's plan, in which case their rejection of God's word results in their ruin. Therefore, they are appointed to God's plan, that those who reject His mercy and grace, refusing to believe upon hearing the Gospel and being convicted by the Holy Spirit, would be condemned to eternal damnation.

The passage cannot be said to support the idea that God is revealing who He decreed to be appointed to condemnation. The condemnation from God resulted because the person was disobedient to God. (See verses 7 and 8) That is what these verses state. Note that the disobedience was followed by condemnation. The passage is not stating that God refused to offer His grace which resulted in the person being elected to be eternally lost. It plainly states the reason for their condemnation was that they were disobedient to God, not because He decreed they would be lost. If God decreed their condemnation He would not have referred to their disobedience as having any significance. God is not the cause of man's disobedience, but it is man's love of sin and refusal to bow in faith to God that brings condemnation.

Another Misused Passage: 1 Peter 2:9

First Peter 2:9 says,

> ". . . But ye are a chosen generation, a royal priesthood, an holy nation, a peculiar people . . ."

The misuse of 1 Peter 2 is another good example of the error of Calvinism. The Calvinist sees the word "chosen" and concludes that this is referring to their view that God in the past decreed in His sovereignty whom He would save and who He would not. They believe that God has chosen who He will allow to receive Him and from whom He will withhold His grace. The ones chosen are the "elect," and the one's not elected, God condemns to the Lake of Fire with no chance of salvation. However, this is a false premise that is not found in God's word.

The Calvinist does not use a correct exegetical approach to interpretation which finds the meaning within the words of the statement. 1 Peter 2:9-10 contextually states what the believer is chosen to, not to who would be chosen. The verse states that the believer is appointed to be a part of a "chosen generation, a royal priesthood, a holy nation, and a peculiar people." Note that each of the words used describes what the believer is chosen to, and not addressing individuals, but groups or classes of saved people. An individual cannot be described as a "chosen generation." A "chosen generation" is not referring to an individual, but people within a time frame. A "royal priesthood" is referring to a class of people. Clearly, a "holy nation" cannot be applied to an individual, but to all believers, and a "peculiar people" is referring to humans considered as a group of indefinite numbers.

1 Peter 2:8-10 exegetically gives no support to Calvinism. Like all the other passages, the Calvinist imposes his false view on these verses to support his faulty human idea. This passage is revealing God's plan; not who would be saved or from whom He would withhold His grace.

Does 2 Peter 1:10-11 support Calvinism?

> *"Wherefore the rather, brethren, give diligence to make your calling and election sure: for if ye do these things, ye shall never fall: For so an entrance shall be ministered unto you abundantly into*

the everlasting kingdom of our Lord and
Saviour Jesus Christ." (2 Peter 1:10-11)

The Calvinists have distorted the meaning of this verse and passage to support the false idea that the "elect" are those specially chosen by God to receive His grace and that only those whom He has predestined can be saved. To find the true meaning of this verse, carefully and exegetically look at the subject and words of the verses.

The context of the passage is shown in verses 1-9,

"Grace and peace be multiplied unto you
through the knowledge of God, and of
Jesus our Lord" (2 Peter 1:2)

Grace and peace abounds to those who recognize (epignoss) acknowledge and know God and Jesus our Lord. Verses 3-4 reveal that through God's power he gives the believer everything that pertains to life and godliness. (See Col. 2:10) This completeness in Christ is achieved through our knowledge of Him, in which He calls us to glory and "virtue" (arete) excellence.

Verses 5-7 Peter instruct the believer to live a godly life and note the attributes of godliness. Verses 8-9 say that if the believer has these attributes in his life he will not be barren or fruitless. The one who is blind to these godly attributes has forgotten that God purged his old or past sins.

Verse 10 states:

"Wherefore the rather, brethren, give
diligence to make your calling and
election sure: for if ye do these things, ye
shall never fall" (2 Peter 1:10)

In other words, to ensure you give diligence, or

labor to make sure that you are living what God has called you to, which are the attributes earlier mentioned in verse 8-9. The word "calling" is the word "klesis" and means an invitation. "Eekloge" is translated "election" and means chosen. Therefore the believer is invited (called) and chosen (elected) to live a godly live in Christ Jesus.

This passage, as well as others, shows that election is what God ordained salvation to accomplish and be in the life of the believer. Election does not pertain to who God saves by His grace, but what those who believe will experience by receiving God's grace.

Verse 11, continues saying that if a believer heeds these instructions, he shall be richly supplied (epichoregethesetai) into the everlasting kingdom of our Lord Jesus Christ.[52] (A.T. Robertson. See 1 Thess. 1:9 for use of the word)

Peter sums up the principle saying

> "Wherefore I will not be negligent to put you always in remembrance of these things, though ye know them, and be established in the present truth." (2 Peter 1:12)

The Calvinist uses the passage falsely teaching that it addresses a "professing" Christian and admonishes him to make sure he is saved and one of God's "elect" or chosen. A simple and honest reading shows their error. This verse is written to believers who by their faith in Jesus Christ were saved, and who Peter is admonishing to live a godly life. Verse 9 shows the problem in some believer's lives in that they appear blind to their calling to live a godly life. This disobedient and blind believer has forgotten that his sins were purged, thus plainly this is addressing a saved Christian. The call to godly living is the subject of this passage, not who God chose to be saved, but how the saved should live. This does not support Calvinism's false idea that God elected some to receive His grace and others from whom He with holds grace thus creating them to burn in the fires of hell (Gehenna).

Do passages such as Jeremiah 1:5 support Calvinism?

> *"Before I formed thee in the belly I knew thee; and before thou camest forth out of the womb I sanctified thee, and I ordained thee a prophet unto the nations." (Jeremiah 1:5)*

This verse plainly states that God "knew" Jeremiah. This clearly refers to God's foreknowledge of the birth of Jeremiah and of who and what Jeremiah would be. God then, being omniscient, knew that Jeremiah would be a man of faith and serve Him, and He chose him to be a prophet to Judah and the nations in that area. God says clearly that He chose Jeremiah to be a prophet by His foreknowledge. Foreknowledge is not the same as "fore decreeing." God was not taken by surprise as to what would be Jeremiah's character. If God was telling us He decreed to make Jeremiah a prophet without giving him a choice, why did He not say that? Why did he say He "knew" Jeremiah? Knowing is not the same as decreeing. God is omniscient; He knows all things, including who would be born on earth and how they would live their lives. God knows all men and here emphasizes that He had knowledge of Jeremiah, meaning of his character and faith. God then chose to use a man who would be faithful to him. Again the Calvinist interprets this passage eisegetically, applying his presupposition that God decreed certain ones for salvation and withheld His grace from others. They conclude that God did not give Jeremiah a choice, but forced him to obey His will. Yet the passage does not state that or even suggest that idea. The Calvinist's problem is that he sees everything within the tenants of his false system of theology. His interpretation of God's word will always support his Calvinistic ideas. God is telling us that He "knew" Jeremiah would be a man of faith and that God could use him as a prophet to Israel.

There is no support in this passage for opinions or presuppositions that go beyond what God has stated. Clearly, Calvinists are grabbing at straws when they use Jeremiah or others like John the Baptist, who God chose as His prophets through His foreknowledge, to support their false teaching. This explanation does not fit their erroneous theology, so they reject this truth. The Bible does not teach that God predestined some to Heaven and others to hell. Nowhere in these verses, or anywhere else in God's word, is it stated or implied that God predestined some to salvation and others to go to hell, having no chance to be saved. Those that make such statements have gravely misapplied God's word to their false ideas. What is predestined is God's plan of salvation, that a believer becomes a child of God, the result of salvation, and what the believer's position is with God once they are saved, and the life he then lives in Christ. God's plan is what He predestined. God's plan is that a man who believes in the Lord Jesus Christ is saved, and the one that rejects God's grace is lost and condemns himself.

Believing Calvinism is Believing a Man

When a man believes in Calvinism, it is always the result of accepting the teaching of some other man. Calvinism is only accepted by those to whom it is taught. If a man studies the Bible alone, he will never become a Calvinist. Understanding that God is love and offers grace freely, it would never enter in a Bible student's mind that God would choose to send some individuals to hell and deny them the ability to respond to the Gospel. The Bible's theme which is presented repeatedly is that God is a God of love and grace. Understanding God's unchanging character of love and justice would not allow me to be swayed in that false direction.

Calvinism Extols the Sovereignty of God

Calvinism seems to pride itself in praising and defending the sovereignty of God, which is the premier doctrine of Calvinism. The believer who rejects Calvinism also accepts that God is absolutely sovereign. But God's sovereignty cannot contradict His other attributes. God's attribute of love and justice would not allow Him to deny His grace to untold millions. It would be against God's very nature for Him to do this. Calvinism in reality misrepresents God's nature. He demeans and degrades God's sovereignty, making God unloving and unjust, by saying that God uses His sovereignty unjustly, not allowing some to be saved.

CHAPTER NINE

WHAT DOES THE BIBLE SAY ABOUT SALVATION?

The Bible Commands All Men to Believe

The Scriptures tell us that man must believe in Jesus Christ in order to be saved. There are literally hundreds of Scriptures that teach that man must believe, trust or have faith in God.

> *"For God so loved the world, that he gave his only begotten Son, that whosoever believeth in him should not perish, but have everlasting life." (John 3:16)*
>
> *"For I am not ashamed of the gospel of Christ: for it is the power of God unto salvation to every one that believeth; to the Jew first, and also to the Greek." (Romans 1:16)*
>
> *"Therefore being justified by faith, we have peace with God through our Lord Jesus Christ." (Romans 5:1)*
>
> *"For by grace are ye saved through faith; and that not of yourselves: it is the gift of God: Not of works, lest any man should boast." (Ephesians 2:9)*
>
> *"For after that in the wisdom of God the world by wisdom knew not God, it pleased God by the foolishness of preaching to save them that believe." (1 Corinthians 1:21)*

A man must believe and by faith receive God's

offer of salvation. Belief is an act of man's will. However, man has nothing to boast of in the process of exercising his will and believing what God has said. The act of atonement for sin was accomplished by the Lord Jesus, not man. Suppose you received a gift from someone that offered it to you out of the goodness of their heart. You were not offered the gift because you deserved or had earned it, but because they "willed" or wanted you to have it. In their care or love for you, they wanted you to have something nice. Your act of reaching out and taking the gift does not change it into something you deserved, does it? Would your act of receiving the gift mean you had earned it or paid something for it? Obviously the answer is no; the one who offers the gift decides, within themselves, why they give the gift, not the one who accepts it. The Arminian is right when he states that salvation is entirely the act of a Sovereign God. He is wrong, however, when he concludes that a man in receiving Christ is in some way working for, or meriting salvation. The Calvinist's extreme views are wrong when they take away man's responsibility to receive Christ by stating that God has decreed some to be saved and others to be lost and that grace is irresistible. God rightly commands all men to believe and receive His Son the Lord Jesus Christ as their Savior. A man cannot exercise his will outside the limits that God has set in place. Thus God has, in an act of His will, enabled all men to receive salvation.

The Calvinist is right when he states that salvation is totally the act of a Sovereign God. He is wrong, however, when he concludes that a man in believing and receiving Christ is in some way working for, or meriting salvation. The Calvinist's extreme views are wrong when they take away man's responsibility to receive Christ, by stating that God has decreed some to be saved and others to be lost and that grace is irresistible. God rightly commands all men to believe and receive His Son the Lord Jesus Christ as their Savior.

God Will Not Violate a Man's Will

One important truth that further refutes Calvinism is that God will not violate a man's will. God has not created man as a programmed robot with his life predestined at his creation. In God's plan, He allows man the freedom to choose for himself the course of his life. It was God's sovereign choice to create man with the ability to reason and to love, which are both acts of one's will. Man can respond to God when the Holy Spirit enlightens the man's heart. That happens when a man hears the Gospel or as Romans 1:19-20 states, when man responds to natural revelation that God shows him from nature. God elected the plan of salvation and what He designed it to accomplish. He gave man a will, and in doing so He allows a man to respond to God willingly and in love.

CHAPTER TEN

THE BIBLICAL EXPLANATION

The Trap Set By Human Wisdom

Many believers who accept a literal and holistic interpretation of Scripture have the correct and biblical understanding of the matter, and they reject both the extremes of the Calvinist and Arminian systems. Both the Calvinists and the Arminians have fallen into a trap set by human wisdom, that tries to explain and systematize every act of God. They have used the poorest of hermeneutical principles and reached wrong conclusions about God Himself. God clearly has not told man everything about Himself or given us the "why" of all He has done. But what He has plainly revealed is that we are to believe Him, trust Him, accept Him and live. It is unthinkable that God would leave us in a state of confusion over the matter of salvation! Yet, that is what the Calvinist concludes. All this confusion is not in God's word, but in the unsound reasoning of some men.

God made salvation so simple and clear that even a small child can believe and be saved and become a witness and testimony to others. What is the value of spending countless hours concocting theological systems that seek to second guess all God has done? The Bible principle that "you can know the vine by its fruit" is well applied here. What has been the fruit of Calvinism or Arminianism? They have both led to confusion, division and false teaching. Therefore both systems should be rejected because both produce unbiblical results.

The Attacks By Calvinist Writers

One response of those who hold to extreme views on the doctrine of election is often to condescend to judgmental and cult-like attacks on those who would differ with them. Almost every Calvinist writer I've studied, to some degree, harshly judges the motives of non-Calvinists.

Gordon Clark

Calvinist Gordon Clark descends to criticizing those who differ from the Calvinist view by concluding they are not students of the Bible and not interested in doctrine.[53] That is a meretricious and unscholarly attack on those who disagree with him. A swipe at non-Calvinists establishes nothing and certainly does nothing to support his position or credibility as a Bible scholar. It is a childish response and out of place with biblical scholarship. Many renowned and scholarly men with earned degrees in Bible disagree and reject Calvinism. To say that they are not scholarly or interested in doctrine shows an extremely unsound bias on Clark's part.

The Calvinist C. D. Cole

The Calvinist C. D. Cole makes this harsh judgment toward those who do not accept Calvinism, saying,

> "Ah, the real trouble with the objector is not election; it is something else. His real objection is to total depravity or human inability to do good."[54]

This is simply a false and foolish statement. Most Bible scholars and students who reject to Calvinism accept that man is a sinner lost in his sins as Romans 3:10 plainly states. That means a man is corrupt, wicked, perverted and absolutely not able to save himself. Once again the Calvinist does not offer any real defense of his beliefs but makes a personal attack on those who will not accept his false beliefs using unfounded false critical assertions.

John MacArthur

John MacArthur also fits this mold and accuses objectors to the Calvinistic system as doing so because of pride.[55]

Kenneth Good

Kenneth Good, who falsely places all traditional Baptists as being in the Calvinist camp correctly says,

> "It is to be regretted that both confusion and emotion seem to reign in the current discussions on Calvinism versus Arminianism. Considerably more heat than light is being generated by the energy presently expended in most quarters."[56]

The Calvinist often resorts to defending his position by stating those that reject this false view are rejecting God's sovereignty. That too is an absurd statement. Such a weak defense shows the unsound foundation on which their ideas are founded. Certainly, Almighty God is absolutely sovereign, but that does not preclude that He can go against His own nature. The true biblist correctly understands and accepts God's sovereignty, but this does not mean he must accept the theology of Calvinists which contradicts God's other attributes. The true Bible scholar knows that God in His sovereignty does not violate His own nature or His stated word. Both the Calvinists and the Arminians have taken extreme positions and neither has proved its system to be biblical or a correct explanation of the doctrines of election. Huntsmen, of David Jeremiah's "Turning Point," in a weak attempt to defend Calvinism's contradictions, tells us not to attempt to "reconcile" the teachings of God on election and the sovereignty of God[57]. Both the Calvinist and the Arminian teachings contain some truth, but they go further than God does and that makes them erroneous. I have been a student of the Bible since I was saved in 1972 at 32 years of age. With gratitude, I thank those that taught me that the first distinctive of a New Testament believer was to accept the Bible as my sole authority for faith and practice. The Bible is the authority, not the theological systems of man. I am a Christian, a believer in Jesus Christ and I identify myself totally with Him and Him alone.

Paul condemned the error of identifying oneself with man or religious teachers in 1 Corinthians 1:12. In 1 Corinthians 3:4, Paul says identifying oneself with anyone but Jesus Christ is a carnal act. True believers identify themselves with Jesus Christ, He is the Word, and only His word is Truth. The true believer is to accept God's word, as His only source for his faith and practice. The Calvinist, by accepting John Calvin's *"Institutes"* as their source and explanation of their faith, make a serious mistake.

132

CHAPTER ELEVEN

THE CONCLUSION ON A PERSONAL NOTE

The Author's Rejection of Calvinism and Arminianism

I am not a Calvinist nor am I am Arminian. I reject both titles and theological systems. They both are the heretical and cult-like systems of fallible men. I choose to call myself a Biblicist, or simply a "Bible believer." I identify myself with my Savior and His word. I take no pride in the fact that I am saved, yet I am eternally grateful. I am awed by the truth that the Lord Jesus Christ died on Calvary's cross for my sin. I am deeply and eternally grateful to God who loved this blind sinner that much! I totally reject the idea that I received salvation on any merit of my own! I was, as God said, a sinner, dead in trespasses and sin, sold unto sin, a child of sin, and with no righteousness of my own. I was saved by the sovereign act and plan of our loving God, who came to the earth, incarnate in man and totally paid my sin debt. I did not merit salvation and was totally in bondage to my sinful nature. I absolutely had no spark of divinity in me. Yet, God loved me, His created being, and suffered for me while I was yet in my sin. He provided the way and the means of my salvation by His grace through faith. I am not going to try and put Almighty God in a box and systematize God's act of saving the sinner. I am just going to believe His very Word and thank Him for loving me, the sinner that I am, and forgiving my sin and giving me eternal life.

Man cannot take pride or boast of any merit on his part in his salvation.

> *"For by grace are ye saved through faith; and that not of yourselves: it is the gift of God: Not of works, lest any man should boast" (Ephesians 2:8-9).*

Man cannot merit salvation by good works.

> *"But to him that worketh not, but believeth on him that justifieth the ungodly, his faith is counted for righteousness" (Romans 4:5).*

Man has no goodness or righteousness in him upon which to base his salvation.

> *"But God commendeth his love toward us, in that, while we were yet sinners, Christ died for us." (Romans 5:8)*
> *"For all have sinned, and come short of the glory of God" (Romans 3:23).*

The Failure of Human Rationalization

Many in history have fallen into the trap of going further than Scripture goes and trying, with human rationalization, to explain and systematize God's actions. The result of such rationalization is that most of the time, it leads to extremism. Finite men with finite minds cannot systematize Almighty God! It is an extreme and false view that says God predestined some men to be damned to hell and does not offer them salvation. It is equally an extreme view that states man can in any way merit his salvation or lose the eternal life that God gives the believer.

Each view, whether Calvinism or Arminianism, when adhered to violates clear biblical teaching and therefore cannot be truth. My position is that I reject the extremes of both the Calvinists and the Arminians and I do not use either name in identifying my stand on accepting what the Bible clearly teaches.

The Subject of This Book Is of Great Importance

There was a time in which I did not think that these issues were of a great importance. I have since changed my mind because I have seen the fruit of Calvinism. Over the past years, many people have written and expressed of the confusion and anguish the teachings of Calvinism causes in their lives. One dear lady wrote and said she had not had any children because she was afraid that God would not elect them to salvation[58].

Others instead of accepting the biblical assurance of their salvation, lived in fear of not being among the "elected." Calvinism for these has cast a shadow over their assurance of salvation, because they wondered if they were elected or rejected by God. One man wrote that when his church began teaching Calvinism, he said

"I was sick for two weeks, couldn't sleep or eat. I was bothered by it taking away the loving Savior I had known all my life."[59]

Another young man wrote saying he was seeking the Lord and studying the claims of Christ. He then stumbled across the teachings of Calvinism and said it shattered him. He said,

> "My question to you is, am I able to make a choice to follow Christ? If I want to believe and follow Christ, can I do so? Or is it not my choice? I feel odd trying to put this question into words, but I've tried. The bottom line is, if I wished to become a Christian today, tomorrow or whenever I feel I am ready, can I do so? Calvinists have tried to tell me that I have the inability to call upon Christ, and that if not one of the elect, I won't be saved. Please help!"[60]

For years I have corresponded with Calvinists, and found they will rarely concede to any plain biblical truth that does not agree with their theology. From their statements about the matter and often their insulting attacks, it is my personal conclusion that they seem to be a proud people who see themselves as having a superior intellect and spirituality above those who do not accept their theology. However, their fruit is corrupt because it ignores a great deal of God's word, and worse distorts it even the very nature of God.

Jesus said,

> *"Wherefore by their fruits ye shall know them."* (Matthew 7:20)

BIOGRAPHY

Abrams, III, Cooper P., "*Bible Truth Web Site*," (http://bible-truth.org/Principles.htm).

Arndt, William F. and Gingrich. F. Wilbur. <u>A Greek-English Lexicon of the New Testament</u>. Chicago, University of Chicago, 1957.

Barns, Albert. <u>Albert Barn's Notes on the Bible</u>. Grand Rapids, Baker, 1949.

Bible Truth Web Site, "*Calvinism page, Comments from Readers*". (http:bible-truth.org/Electioncomments.html).

Bouwsma, William J. <u>John Calvin, A Sixteen Century Portrait.</u> New York, Oxford, 1988.

Cairns, Earle E. <u>Christianity Through the Centuries</u>. Grand Rapids, Zondervan, 1967.

John Calvin. <u>The Institutes of the Christian Religion</u> [1537] Translated by Henry Beveridge. (John Calvin. <u>The Institutes of the Christian Religion</u> (Kindle Locations 2-3)).

_____. The Institutes of the Christian Religion, A New Translation by Henry Beveridge, Esq,

_____. <u>(2010-02-19). The Institutes of the Christian Religion (Kindle Location 100). . Kindle Edition.</u>

_____. (2011-11-24). Calvin's Calvinism: A Treatise on the Eternal Predestination of God. Translated by Henry Cole. (Kindle Locations 190-192). . Kindle Edition.

Bernard Cottret. Calvin A Biography. Eerdmans, Grand Rapids, 2000. (Kindle Location 2304). Kindle Edition.

Harkness, Georgia. John Calvin, The Man and His Ethics. New York, Abingdon Press, 1958.

Hull, William. On Calvinism, LONDON: PRINTED FOR J. G. F. & J. RIVINGTON,
1841, (Kindle Location 17) Public Domain Books. Kindle Edition.

Huntsman, Gene, Letter dated April, 18, 2001, from, Dr. David Jeremiah, "Turning Point," . PO Box 3838, San Diego, CA 92163.

Jeremiah, David. God Loves You, He Always Has, He Always Will. New York, Faith Words, 2012.

Kingdon, Robert M.. Adultery and Divorce in Calvin's Geneva. Cambridge, Harvard University Press, 1995.

Niesel, Wilhelm. The Theology of Calvin, Translated by Harold Knight. Philadelphia, Westminister Press, 1956.

Parker, T.H.L.. <u>John Calvin, A Biography</u>. Philadelphia, Westminister Press, 1975

Schaff, Phillip. <u>New Schaff-Herzog Encyclopedia of Religious Knowledge, Vol. X: . Reutsch - Son</u>, Baker, Grand Rapid, 1953.

Steele, David N. Thomas, Curtis C., Quinn, S. Lance. <u>The Five Points of Calvinism, 2nd Edition</u> Phillipsburg, NJ, P&R Publishing Company, 1962.
Walker, Williston <u>John Calvin, The Organizer of Reformed Protestantism</u>, New York, The Knickerbocker Press, 1096.

Stefan Zweig. *Erasmus; The Right to Heresy: Castellio against Calvin* . London, Cassell, 1951.

INDEX OF WORDS & PHRASES

ABOUT THE AUTHOR

Cooper Abrams and wife, Carolyn

Dr. Cooper Abrams is the pastor of Calvary Baptist Church, Tremonton, Utah. He is a veteran missionary, pastor, church planter, and author working in the state of Utah since 1986. He and his wife Carolyn are missionaries sent by Calvary Baptist Church, King, NC and have been involved in seeing three sound Independent Baptist churches established in Utah since 1986.

He graduated from Piedmont Baptist College in 1981 with a Th.B. (Bachelor of Theology), and in 2000 with an MBS (Master of Biblical Studies).   In 2013, he earned a Ph.D in Religion - Bible Major from Bethany Divinity College and Seminary.

He is an avid writer and has authored numerous articles, books, Bible courses, and six Bible commentaries.   He has written many articles on apologetics, hermeneutics, Baptist History, The Pentecostal Movement, and Mormonism.

Most of his work is posted on his popular Internet website, Bible Truth **http://bible-truth.org**. The website which was begun in 1996 currently averages over sixty-five hundred visitors per day. The site is rated between the top two to five Baptist websites, out of thousands, on the "Baptist Top 1000", the "Independent Fundamental 1000," and the "Fundamental 500."

He can be contacted at:
PO Box 304
Tremonton, Utah 84337
435 452-1716
Email: cpabrams3@gmail.com

ENDNOTES

1. Biblist is one who holds the Bible as his sole authority for his faith and practice.

2. Calvin, John. *Institutes of the Christian Religion, A New Translation by Henry Beveridge, Esq.*, Kindle Locations 99-100, Kindle Edition.

3. T.H.L. Parker, *John Calvin, A Biography*, Philadelphia, Westminister Press, 1975, p. 13.

4. *Licentiate*: the holder of a university degree intermediate between that of a bachelor and doctor degree who has received a license to practice an art or profession.

5. William J. Bouwsma, *John Calvin, a Sixteen-Century Portrait*, New York, Oxford Press, 1988, p. 11.

6. Parker, 22.

7. Patrick Collinson, *The Reformation: A History*, New York, Random House, 2003, p. 88.

8. There are two Talmuds, the Jerusalem and the Babylonian.

9. Also see Rom. 6:15, 7:1-25; 9:31-32, 10:4-6; Gal.5:18.

10. Robert M. Kingdon, *Adultery and Divorce in*

Calvin's Geneva, Cambridge, Harvard University Press, 1995, p. 10.

11. Ibid.

12. Georgia Harkness, *John Calvin, The Man and His Ethics* , New York, Abingdon Press, 1958, p. 21.

13. Ibid.

14. Harkness, p. 22.

15. Phillip Schaff, *New Schaff-Herzog Encyclopedia of Religious Knowledge*, Vol. X: Reutsch - Son, Baker, Grand Rapid, 1953, p. 371.

16. Walter Nigg, *The Heretics* , New York, Alfred A. Knopf, Inc., 1962, p. 328.

17. Nigg, p. 327.

18. Nigg, p. 328.

19. Bernard Cottret, *Calvin A Biography*, Eerdmans, Grand Rapids, 2000, p. 180.

20. Selderhuis, Herman J., *John Calvin   A Pilgrim's Life,* Downer's Grove, IL, InterVarity Press. 2009, p. 139-140.

21. Cottret, Kindle Locations 2315-2316

22. Ibid.

23. Mr. Bernard Cottret. *Calvin: A Biography*, Kindle Locations 1050-1051, Kindle Edition, 2000.

24. Calvin, John . *Calvin's Calvinism: A Treatise on the Eternal Predestination of God*. Translated by Henry Cole, pp.179, 182. Kindle Locations 1337-1341.

25. *Calvin's Calvinism*, Kindle Locations 1337-1341, Kindle Edition

26. Cole, 26.

27. John Calvin. The Institutes of the Christian Religion (Kindle Locations 23496-23498).

28. John Calvin (2010-02-19). The Institutes of the Christian Religion (Kindle Location 17699). Kindle Edition.

29. Ibid

30. *Calvin's Calvinism*, Kindle Locations pp. 190-192.

31. Stefan Zweig, *Erasmus; The Right to Heresy: Castellio against Calvin*, London, Cassell, 1951, p. 234.

32. Mr. Bernard Cottret. *Calvin: A Biography* (Kindle Locations 1635-1637). Kindle Edition

33. Cottret, Kindle Locations 2138-2139, Kindle Edition.

34. Cottret, Kindle Locations 1788-1790, Kindle Edition.

35. Cottret, Kindle Locations 1811-1812, Kindle Edition.

36. Ibid.

37. C. D. Cole, *Definitions of Doctrines, Vol. 2, Chapter 3, Election*, Lexington,KY, Byran Station Baptist Church, p.1968.

38. John Mac Arthur, Jr., *Chosen for Eternity: A Study of Election*, "Grace to You", Panorama City, CA, 1989 9-10.

39. Ibid., p 9.

40. Gene Huntsman, *Letter dated April, 18, 2001*, Dr. David Jeremiah, "Turning Point", PO Box 3838, San Diego, CA 92163, p. 1.

41. Huntsman, p2.

42. Gordon H. Clark, *Biblical Predestination*, Presbyterian and Reformed Publishing Co., Phillipsburg, New Jersey, 1969, pp.2-4.

43. Cole, Part I.

44. MacArthur, p.9.

45. William F Arndt, and F. Wilbur Gingrich, *A Greek-English Lexicon of the New Testament,*

Chicago, University of Chicago, 1957, p. 446.

46. Jeremiah, David (2012-10-04). God Loves You: He Always Has--He Always Will (Kindle Locations 57-61). Hachette Book Group. Kindle Edition.

47. Desiring God. John Piper. 2009. http://www.desiringgod.org/resource-library/sermons /god-so-loved-the-world-part-1.

48. Desiring God. John Piper. 2009. Piper, John. http://www.desiringgod.org/blog/posts/is-gods-love-unconditional.

49. Cooper P. Abrams, III, "*Bible Truth Web Site*," http://bible-truth.org/Principles.htm.

50. Lewis Sperry Chafer, *Systematic Theology, Vol. III. Soteriology,* Dallas Seminary Press, Dallas, Texas, 1948, p. 188.

51. Albert Barnes, *Barnes New Testament Notes*, Baker:Grand Rapids, Reprint 1884-85 Edition, Blackie and Sons, London, p. 191.

52. A.T. Robertson. *A. T. Robertson's Word Pictures*, See 1 Thess. 1:9 for use of the word.

53. Clark, p..

54. Huntsman, p. 2.

55. Cooper Abrams, *Bible Truth Web Site*, http://bible-truth.org/ Electioncomments.html

56. Good, p 52.

57. Huntsman.

58. Abrams, *Comments*.

59. Ibid.

60. Ibid.

CPSIA information can be obtained
at www.ICGtesting.com
Printed in the USA
LVOW03s1333250218
567809LV00034B/2223/P